Happiness

This book introduces the reader to the ways in which happiness has been explored in philosophy and literature for thousands of years, in order to understand the newest theoretical approaches to happiness.

Jeffrey R. Di Leo draws on its long and rich history as a window into our present obsession with happiness. Each of the four chapters of this book provides a substantially different literary-theoretical account of how and why literature matters with respect to considerations of happiness. From the neoliberal happiness industry and the psychoanalytic rejection of happiness to aesthetic hedonism and revolutionary happiness, literature viewed from the perspective of happiness becomes a story about what is and is not the goal of life.

The multidisciplinary approach of this book will appeal to a variety of readers from literary studies, critical theory, philosophy and psychology and anyone with an interest in happiness and theories of emotion.

Jeffrey R. Di Leo is Professor of English and Philosophy at the University of Houston-Victoria, USA. He is editor and publisher of the *American Book Review*, founder and editor of the journal *symplokē*, and Executive Director of the Society for Critical Exchange and its Winter Theory Institute.

New Literary Theory
Series editors: Andy Mousley and Jeff Wallace

Just Literature
Philosophical Criticism and Justice
Tzachi Zamir

Happiness
Jeffrey R. Di Leo

For more information about this series, please visit: www.routledge.com/New-Literary-Theory/book-series/NLTH

Happiness

Jeffrey R. Di Leo

LONDON AND NEW YORK

First published 2022
by Routledge
4 Park Square, Milton Park, Abingdon, Oxon OX14 4RN

and by Routledge
605 Third Avenue, New York, NY 10158

Routledge is an imprint of the Taylor & Francis Group, an informa business

© 2022 Jeffrey R. Di Leo

The right of Jeffrey R. Di Leo to be identified as author of this work has been asserted in accordance with sections 77 and 78 of the Copyright, Designs and Patents Act 1988.

All rights reserved. No part of this book may be reprinted or reproduced or utilised in any form or by any electronic, mechanical, or other means, now known or hereafter invented, including photocopying and recording, or in any information storage or retrieval system, without permission in writing from the publishers.

Trademark notice: Product or corporate names may be trademarks or registered trademarks, and are used only for identification and explanation without intent to infringe.

British Library Cataloguing-in-Publication Data
A catalogue record for this book is available from the British Library

Library of Congress Cataloging-in-Publication Data
Names: Di Leo, Jeffrey R., author.
Title: Happiness / Jeffrey R. Di Leo.
Description: Abingdon, Oxon; New York, NY: Routledge, 2022. |
Series: Newliterary theory | Includes bibliographical references
and index.
Identifiers: LCCN 2021037789 (print) | LCCN 2021037790 (ebook) |
ISBN 9781032015200 (hardback) | ISBN 9781032015224 (paperback) |
ISBN 9781003178941 (ebook)
Subjects: LCSH: Happiness. | Well-being. | Happiness in
literature.
Classification: LCC BF575.H27 D524 2022 (print) |
LCC BF575.H27 (ebook) | DDC 152.4/2—dc23
LC record available at https://lccn.loc.gov/2021037789
LC ebook record available at https://lccn.loc.gov/2021037790

ISBN: 978-1-032-01520-0 (hbk)
ISBN: 978-1-032-01522-4 (pbk)
ISBN: 978-1-003-17894-1 (ebk)

DOI: 10.4324/9781003178941

Typeset in Times New Roman
by codeMantra

Know happiness.

—Samuel Beckett

Contents

New Literary Theory

Series Preface

Why does or should literature matter to us? What is its value and significance for human existence in the twenty-first century? *New Literary Theory* aims to breathe new life into the way we think about literature. The books in the series will be erudite but not narrowly specialist, informed by up-to-date research but not overburdened by scholarly reference. The spirit of the series is to emulate the vitality, experimentalism and freedom of literature itself, and to find fresh and accessible ways of writing about our engagements with it.

The re-focusing of attention upon the particularities of literature is not intended to be nostalgic or defensive. The series will encourage a plurality of approaches to 'the literary' and will not seek to prescribe what literary studies now is or might become in an era of revolutionary cultural transformation in which the conditions for reading texts as 'literature' are drastically changing, if not disappearing. For 'literature' consists not simply in its sources of value—works of art and their creators—but in the reading formations and institutions that make the concept of literature possible: textual literacy; the possibility of the individual's sustained, private encounter with the text, or time and space to read in an undistracted way; an educational system in which to teach the concept of the literary. Books, the market activists tell us, are still alive and well but are their readers still out there and, if so, for how long? The reorientation of human consciousness in 'developed' societies and the monopolisation of attention and concentration through digital technology, screens, mobile phones, and social media is occurring with extraordinary rapidity.

Our rationale for reinvigorating and re-imagining the literary is in part provoked by the implications of these far-reaching cultural changes. But it can simultaneously be traced back to the historical and conceptual drift between 'literary theory' and the thing that became 'theory'. The revolution in literary studies from the 1960s onwards was fired by an initial interest in the theory of what literature is and does, gathered from various twentieth-century sources—from, say, Russian formalism, through New Criticism, stylistics, structuralism and narratology to post-structuralism. But then 'theory' detached itself, becoming no longer simply a concern with the literary as such, but a way of reading literature in and through philosophy, psychology, and psychoanalysis, movements of political thought and activism, and frameworks of ethical value. The series will build upon each of these aspects of 'literary/theory', acknowledging their immeasurable enrichment of literary studies as a mode of intellectual work. Yet we are also eager to (re)focus attention on what it means to think concertedly 'with literature' about any given field of enquiry.

There has been a tendency also for the teaching of literary theory in undergraduate programmes to become routinised, with undergraduate modules delivering literary theory as a 'toolkit' of critical approaches that bleach out the historical contexts or political motivations and struggles behind such approaches. The perceived obligation to master and deploy literary-theoretical languages did, inevitably, lead to new kinds of professional performance in critical writing, perhaps sometimes neglectful of the need to keep what was once called, most notably by Virginia Woolf, the intelligent 'common reader', alert and awake. In this sense, the academicisation of theory could seem to be at odds with its emancipatory promise. Resistance to such tendencies means trying to assimilate theory with those more 'common' terms in which readers and students might want to register their engagements with literary texts—emotion and evaluation, perplexity and enlightenment, loving and hating.

Andy Mousley and Jeff Wallace

Acknowledgements

My primary debt of gratitude goes out to Andy Mousley and Jeff Wallace, the editors of this series, for encouraging me to compose a manuscript on happiness for their new series. I appreciate the time, care, and attention that they have afforded this project and consider both model series editors.

During the course of this project, I have benefited from the timely suggestions and insightful conversations of many individuals that have challenged and inspired the work in this volume in various ways: Jacob Blevins, Christopher Breu, Robin Goodman, Peter Hitchcock, Sophia McClennen, Paul Allen Miller, Christian Moraru, John Mowitt, Daniel T. O'Hara, Brian O'Keeffe, Jean-Michel Rabaté, Kenneth Saltman, Nicole Simek, Henry Sussman, Harold Aram Veeser, and Zahi Zalloua.

A special note of appreciation goes out to Polly Dodson of Routledge for her support of this project; to Orlando Di Leo for his editorial assistance; to Vikki Fitzpatrick for securing materials used for the development of this book; and to John Fizer, Bruce Wilshire, and John Yolton, three of my dearly departed philosophical mentors from Rutgers University, who encouraged my theoretical pluralism.

And finally, I would like to thank my wife, Nina, for her unfailing encouragement, support, and patience.

Introduction

Happiness is often touted as the goal of life. It has been pondered in philosophy and explored in literature for thousands of years. This book will present some of these ideas but only in the context of pursuing some new literary theoretical approaches to this very old topic. While this book is not a history of happiness in literature and philosophy, it draws on pieces from its long and rich history as a window into our present obsession with happiness, which today has become nothing less than an industry.

The 'happiness industry'[1] is geared toward the production of goods aimed at increasing it not just in individual lives but also in the workplace and the world at large. For the latter, consider that some countries now have moved from measurement of Gross National Product to Gross National Happiness as the measure of the health of their nation. In the workplace, many companies now employ Chief Happiness Officers whose task it is to monitor and improve employee happiness relative to the workplace. And in individual life, we now have smart technology that strives to cater to every aspect of our personal well-being.

Chapter 1, 'The Brave New World of Well-Being', is a survey of some of these developments in business, psychology, finance, marketing, and smart technology. It also notes the legacy of the work of Émile Chartier, whose contributions to the literature and philosophy of happiness form an important chapter in the commodification of happiness. As happiness is now a product that occupies the forces of many different industries including the national defence and security industries, it should not be surprising that happiness can be viewed as having a role in the production of literature as well. In fact, from the perspective of the happiness industry, it might be argued that the *only* literature that matters is literature that contributes to our happiness

DOI: 10.4324/9781003178941-1

and well-being.[2] This powerful claim affords literature a central role in the happiness industry—albeit, as we will see in the next chapter, much to the chagrin of opponents to this type of use of literature in society.

In 1932, Aldous Huxley published his literary vision of a future society, *Brave New World*. It depicted a controlled state where art and beauty are replaced by comfort and happiness. In the first chapter, Huxley's novel and its non-fiction follow-up, *Brave New World Revisited*, which was published in 1958, are drawn upon as literary and non-literary backdrops for how and why literature matters in the age of the happiness industry. By 1958, the 'dictatorship' of 'happiness' drugs like *Brave New World*'s 'soma' is already no longer a fantasy. The tranquillisers and stimulants imagined in a work of dystopian literature would be developed over the ensuing half-century to the point where opioid addiction today is an epidemic. Is Opiod Literature then the official literature of Prozac nation? Or does the happiness industry have other ideas for literature?

Chapter 2, 'Happiness, No Thanks!', traces a theoretical counter-narrative to the happiness industry and its products. It is one that begins with the invention of psychoanalysis by Sigmund Freud at the turn of the century. Here we find a theory grounded upon the rejection of happiness. In its place, Freud developed the concept of the 'death drive'. He argues that while unhappiness is readily attainable, happiness *is not*. To expect otherwise goes against the fundamental tenets of psychoanalysis. This position will be picked up and developed mid-century by Jacques Lacan, who combines Freud's insights on happiness along with aspects of Ferdinand de Saussure's linguistics to develop a distinctive form of psychoanalysis that makes contributions to poststructuralism, cultural studies, and literary and film theory. But, as we will see, key elements of both Freud and Lacan's psychoanalytic arguments against happiness are grounded in readings of both Greek philosophy and literature.

Today, however, the psychoanalytic tradition of rejecting happiness established by Freud and Lacan is continued in the writings of Slavoj Žižek. One of Žižek's major arguments is that we must reject the pursuit of happiness. This chapter surveys some of Žižek's arguments as well as those of Freud and Lacan. It also provides an overview of some of the major philosophical positions on happiness that these psychoanalytic theorists use as critical fuel for their arguments. Because of the central role of Sophocles's *Oedipus the King* in the formation of psychoanalytic arguments against happiness, the play is foregrounded in this chapter.

Also, we return in Chapter 2 to *Brave New World* and look more closely at the role of psychoanalysis in the formation of Huxley's dystopia of happiness. In short, literature matters for this line of theory only to the extent that it disabuses us of the pursuit of happiness. While psychoanalysis is not a new line of theory, foregrounding the rejection of happiness in a world where happiness is king *is* a brave new—and important—path for theory. Moreover, the theoretical rejection of happiness arguably alters the reputation of literature devoted to the pursuit of happiness. Whereas unlike, say, the eighteenth century, where philosophy and literature were widely viewed as *partners* in the pursuit of happiness, in the twenty-first century, theory and literature appear as *adversaries* regarding happiness: theory works to help us overcome the quest for happiness, while the happiness industry (and its spirtualised hedonism) embraces literature as a primary vehicle of well-being—and book sales.

Chapter 3, 'The Happiness of the Text', examines the late literary theory of Roland Barthes, where he announces his turn to hedonism. Barthes does this with a full awareness that he stood alone among the literary theorists and philosophers of his time (and now ours) in his explicit engagement with the hedonic tradition. Two works in particular, *The Pleasure of the Text*, which he published in 1973, and *Roland Barthes by Roland Barthes*, which was published in 1975, develop this hedonism, which becomes the final phase of Barthes's theoretical development. Though hedonism is generally associated with the pursuit of pleasure as the goal of life, Barthes describes it as a state of comfort. It is one in which particular forms of reading and writing establish a foundation to this comfort. As such, Barthes's hedonism is very different from what Žižek describes as the 'spiritualized hedonism' of our own era, that is, one where happiness is regarded as the supreme duty. While Žižek utilizes the spiritualisation of hedonism as a negative descriptor of the ways in which neoliberal capitalism leads people into a false sense of happiness or well-being, Barthes turns to both a more historically distant sense of hedonism as the 'art de vivre' and couples it with his own hedonism as 'art de textualité' to provide an aesthetic vision of the pursuit of comfort wherein reading and writing have a central role.

One of the major influences on Barthes's hedonism is André Gide. It is widely acknowledged that his journals are his greatest achievement as a writer and were a primary reason he was awarded the Nobel Prize in Literature in 1947. Gide's journals appeared during his lifetime in both periodicals and book form, and were one of the major vehicles of his aesthetic hedonism. So too were several of his early novels, including *The Immoralist*, which he finished in 1901, a year after Freud's *The Interpretation of Dreams*. Because of the role of Gide's work in the development of Barthes's hedonism, both his journals and *The Immoralist* will be discussed in this chapter. Finally, this chapter also provides an overview of some of the major philosophical positions on hedonism dating back to ancient Greece, which is something that seems necessary given that Barthes claims that it is a 'repressed' tradition.

Chapter 4, 'Real Happiness is Revolutionary', turns to an account of happiness that aims to establish a progressive, if not also *revolutionary*, conception of happiness. This is particularly important in a milieu where happiness has been both co-opted by industry *and* rejected by psychoanalysis. The key theorist here is Alain Badiou, who has formulated a metaphysics of happiness that is rooted in what is called 'affect' theory, particularly as introduced by Baruch Spinoza. Spinoza saw the emotions as something that could be studied in the same way that we study geometry or physics. Happiness, for Spinoza, is linked with freeing ourselves from the bondage of our passive emotions, and the attainment of knowledge of our place in the universe. This knowledge shows us why things happen in the ways they do happen and cannot be otherwise. For Spinoza, this brings us both happiness and salvation.

Badiou, following Spinoza's lead, argues that happiness is the infallible sign of all access to truth. However, he also acknowledges, that happiness requires a wager like the one made by Stéphane Mallarmé in *A Throw of the Dice*, which first appeared in 1897. As we will see, Mallarmé's Wager connects back to the original wager that was made by Blaise Pascal. Moreover, following Sören Kierkegaard, Badiou also argues that a certain dose of despair is the condition of real happiness. In Badiou's philosophy, happiness is not an abstract idea of a good society in which everyone is satisfied such as the one developed in *Brave New World*. Rather, happiness is possible by discovering beneath the dull and dreary existence of our world luminous possibilities. In short, for Badiou, we can change the world simply by being happy.

The literary analogue to Badiou's happiness is exemplified in the late literature of Samuel Beckett, where characters enveloped in dull and dreary existences find happiness. Thus, the final literary work that we will turn to here is one of Beckett's last and most beautiful, *Ill Seen Ill Said*, which was first published in 1981. It closes with the immortal line that stands as the epigraph to this book: 'Know happiness'.

This study assesses how happiness can inform considerations of the literary at the present moment. Given that each of the four chapters of this book provides a substantially different literary-theoretical account of how and why literature matters with respect to considerations of happiness, the book as a whole stresses the important role of theory in any determination of literature's limits and standing. Literature is never one thing or another but dependent on constructions of its status and value, including theoretical/philosophical ones. From the neoliberal happiness industry and the psychoanalytic rejection of happiness to aesthetic hedonism and revolutionary happiness, literature viewed from the perspective of happiness becomes a story not only about what is and is not the goal of life, but also about the current character of the literary itself with respect to happiness. This story takes us backward to the formative thoughts and lofty expectations for happiness of the ancient Greeks of the fourth and fifth centuries and forward to a brave new world where the topic of dystopian literature has become everyday reality. In the process, the standing of literature today appears as Janus-faced: on one side is literature that is supported by an industry invested in the pursuit of happiness that Barthes would describe as 'readerly'; on the other is a literature whose roots are in the modernist tradition of Gide, Beckett, and Mallarmé, where theoretical considerations complicate happiness to the point where it transforms into an aesthetic hedonism and revolutionary philosophy through literature that Barthes would describe as 'writerly'.

Moreover, what makes happiness such a powerful new tool for literary theory is its interdisciplinary approach to literature. It is an approach where philosophical, psychological, scientific, political, and business concerns are often called upon to gain insight on literary ones. If happiness in literature were only about identifying stories with happy endings or happy characters or happy plots, there would be little use for the sister arts and sciences to aid us in this endeavour.

Finally, if we take Beckett's injunction to 'Know happiness' seriously, then the path to this knowledge though literature is a much richer and rewarding one than merely identifying stories that end with 'and they lived happily ever after'. It involves a journey where our epistemological and metaphysical assumptions about happiness are tempered by social, political, and economic concerns. Ultimately, to 'Know happiness' is no less difficult or deep than to 'Know thyself'. If the latter was Socrates's imperative for the philosophical life in ancient Greece, then the former is perhaps the imperative for literary-theoretical life in the new millennium.

Notes

1. See Davies (2015).
2. A distinction has been made by some between 'happiness', which is reserved only for states of mind or psychological matters, and 'well-being', which is used only for value-notions such as what benefits a person or a life that goes well for you (see, for example, Haybron 2013: 11). However, others such as McMahon (2006), regard happiness as a value-notion, that is, in the sense of well-being. This study, however, will distinguish the uses of both terms as appropriate depending on the context of their use.

1 The brave new world of well-being

Happiness as a commodity from Huxley and Alain to Pharrell and Oprah

What would you call a world where 'People are happy; they get what they want, and they never want what they can't get' (Huxley 2006: 220)? A world where 'if anything should go wrong', there's a surefire way to make us to forget about it? In 1932, amidst the rise of Fascism in Western Europe and a world shaken by massive economic depression, a 40-year-old British novelist addressed this question with a power and prophecy that almost a century later reads like a guidebook to selling happiness in the new millennium.

The author was the prolific Aldous Huxley, who, in addition to novels, wrote poetry, plays, short stories, essays, criticism, and philosophy. The novel, *Brave New World*, is one that is on a short list of socially prophetic twentieth-century fiction along with George Orwell's 1949 novel, *Nineteen Eighty-Four*. In fact, when Orwell published *Nineteen Eighty-Four*, he had his publisher send Huxley a copy. Huxley found it a 'profoundly important' (Huxley 1969: 604) book, writing to Orwell:

> Within the next generation I believe that the world's rulers will discover that infant conditioning and narco-hypnosis are more efficient, as instruments of government, than clubs and prisons, and that the lust for power can be just as completely satisfied by suggesting people into loving [sic] their servitude as by flogging and kicking them into obedience. In other words, I feel that the nightmare of *Nineteen Eighty-Four* is destined to modulate into the nightmare of a world having more resemblance to that which I imagined in *Brave New World*. The change will be brought about as a result of a felt need for increased efficiency.
>
> (Huxley 1969: 605)

Nineteen Eighty-Four warns about the terrors of totalitarian government and has become a handbook of modern political abuse. Terms

DOI: 10.4324/9781003178941-2

like Big Brother, Newspeak, Doublethink, Thoughtcrime, and the Thought Police from *Nineteen Eighty-Four* are regularly associated with real-life situations where totalitarian-trending police states abuse their power. Today, for example, when our privacy is invaded through government or corporate technological surveillance, Orwell's 'Big Brother' is often cited to indicate its abuse of political power. Moreover, popular culture has done an ample job in reinforcing and reminding us of the political nightmare depicted in Orwell's *Nineteen Eighty-Four*.

A few years after its publication, there were two television movie adaptations of the novel. In the United States, CBS adapted *Nineteen Eighty-Four* for television in 1953 (Orwell 1953), and in the United Kingdom, BBC adapted it for television in 1954 (Orwell 1954). A few years later, allegedly with 'secret' funding from the United States government (in specific, the Central Intelligence Agency [Morris 2012]), a British film version was made and released in the United Kingdom and the United States (Orwell 1956). Later, it was again brought to the big screen in a 1984 film adaptation (Orwell 1984) with a best-selling soundtrack done by the Eurythmics (Eurythmics 1984), which was followed up with a 2005 operatic version (Maazel 2005) and a 2013 play adaptation (Orwell 2013) with extreme torture scenes that elicited fainting and vomiting among audiences (Lee 2017). Also, it would be remiss not to mention eponymous albums by Yusef Lateef (Lateef 1965), Van Halen (Van Halen 1984), and Rick Wakeman (Wakeman 1981), among others, and eponymous singles by Spirit (Spirit 1969), David Bowie (Bowie 1974a), and Oingo Boingo (Oingo Boingo 1983), and more, all taking their musical inspiration from Orwell's novel. And finally, speaking of Bowie, he originally intended his entire 1974 album *Diamond Dogs* (Bowie 1974b), which includes the aforementioned eponymous single, to be a rock musical based on *Nineteen Eighty-Four*.

But, if Huxley is right, and the totalitarian nightmare of *Nineteen Eighty-Four* 'is destined to modulate into the nightmare of a world having more resemblance to that which [he] imagined in *Brave New World*', then what might this world look like as represented by the other arts? Curiously, unlike Orwell's novel, Huxley's dystopia of happiness is far less the subject of the popular imagination. While there was a radio broadcast of it for the CBS Radio Workshop in 1956 that was narrated by Huxley, there were no accompanying film productions in the United States or the United Kingdom until 1980. Since 2008, however, the BBC has annually broadcast a ten-part reading of *Brave New World* (Huxley 2008) and, in 2016, aired a dramatic production of the novel (Huxley 2016). There was also a staged dramatic adaptation of it, but again, only fairly recently—in 2015 (Huxley 2015). To date, there is no cinematic film adaptation of *Brave New World*, and only two television movie versions—one in 1980 (Huxley 1980) and one in 1998 (Huxley 1998). The director Ridley Scott and the actor Leonardo DiCaprio were said to be developing it as a theatrical film, but to date, the project is on hold. Says Scott of the project,

> I don't know what to do with *Brave New World*. It's tough. I think *Brave New World* in a funny kind of way was good in nineteen thirty-eight, because it had a very interesting revolutionary idea. Don't forget it came shortly before or after George Orwell, roughly the same time. When you re-analyse it, maybe it should stay as a book.
>
> (Weintraub 2012)

This 'revolutionary idea' that Scott says should stay as literature is Huxley's critique of happiness in *Brave New World*.

Nonetheless, in spite of the relative scarcity of adaptations of *Brave New World*, the difficulty of creatively envisioning it in the other arts might not be about the limits of artistic representation. Rather, it may be one about the limits of a *critique* of happiness *in any art*. While Westerners can easily imagine the evils of a government or industry that invades our privacy in the pursuit of total political power, it is much more difficult to depict the 'horrors' of a government which seeks to make everyone maximally happy. The latter is particularly true in the West where the pursuit of happiness is completely ingrained in and celebrated by our culture—if not also, in our way of living. Huxley's *Brave New World* builds a government upon the premise that one of the absolute goods of society is the pursuit of happiness. The artistic challenge here is to get an audience to believe that governmental control in support of maximising social and personal happiness can ever be a bad thing. That is to say, to get an audience to see that *not* getting what you want is ever preferable to getting *everything* that you want. While Huxley's novel is built upon the premise that a society solely dedicated to the maximization of happiness could only be an object of critique and horror, the Western world today finds much of what is fictionalized here to be acceptable.

In *Brave New World*, people *are* happy. They *always* get what they want—not just what they need. It is a stable world where everyone is safe and well off. Moreover,

> they're not afraid of death; they're blissfully ignorant of passion and old age; they're plagued with no mothers or fathers; they've

> got no wives, or children, or lovers to feel strongly about; they're so conditioned that they practically can't help behaving as they ought to behave.
>
> (Huxley 2006: 220)

And, if anything should go wrong, there is a governmentally distributed drug that cures their unhappiness. Huxley calls it 'soma'. In short, this is what Huxley believed awaits us *after* Orwell's totalitarian state: happiness.

Still, the price of happiness is extreme in Huxley's novel. The novel itself questions whether the benefits of complete happiness in modern civilised society are worth its costs. Moreover, in Huxley's novel, happiness has become a commodity. In turn, one of the prophecies of *Brave New World* is that in the future—a future *after* the totalitarian state—happiness will be bought and sold. This chapter will look at both the practice of selling happiness in philosophy, popular music, and psychology, and weigh them against the warnings of Huxley in *Brave New World* about the social and political consequences of commodifying happiness. In the end, what Huxley intended as a social and political satire about the future of happiness in our world has almost become the cookbook for its current status in society. Moreover, because of its iconic literary reputation, *Brave New World* is a good fictional focal point for some of the new theoretical approaches to happiness. But before there was *soma*, there was a widely read French philosopher who offered daily drug-free cures for unhappiness. Let's turn to him next.

One must vow

'It is not difficult to be unhappy or discontented', wrote the philosopher Émile Chartier. 'All you have to do is sit down, like a prince waiting to be amused', he continues. 'This attitude of lying in wait and weighing happiness as if it were a commodity casts the gray shadow of boredom over everything' (Alain 1989: 247).

Chartier was a French philosopher who died in 1951 at the age of 83. He spent his entire professional career teaching philosophy in secondary schools. Though his star has dimmed over the years, while he was alive, he was *the* philosopher of French radicalism. He was also considered by the French in his day as the most important philosopher since France's national philosopher, René Descartes. Chartier's pupils included Raymond Aron, Simone de Beauvoir, Georges Canguilhem, André Maurois, Maurice Schuman, and Simone Weil

(Plottel 2006: 379). He has been called the greatest teacher of their generation (Hellman 1982: 8).

'The key to [Chartier's] teaching', writes John Hellman, 'was his determination to instill critical habits of mind in his students' (Hellman 1982: 8). 'He believed', continues Hellman, 'that students did not truly "acquire" ideas until they had digested them and re-expressed them in their own words'. Rather than in-class exams, he thus preferred to assign '"topos", or take-home essay examinations, to his students which forced them to formulate their own (not "correct") answers to knotty questions' (Hellman 1982: 8).

To be sure, Chartier's pedagogical prowess was as legendary as some of his pupils. Still, the work of his closest contemporary, Henri Bergson, is much more highly regarded today than that of Chartier. Part of the reason is the ephemeral nature of the majority of his writing. That is, while Chartier published numerous books on philosophical topics, he was best known in France through the thousands of articles he published in various daily newspapers. Beginning in 1903, he started to publish these philosophical articles under the pseudonym 'Alain', a name he took from the fifteenth-century Norman poet, Alain Chartier.

At first, Alain's articles were longer weekly columns, and then in 1906, they became daily short articles. The shorter articles were published as a daily column entitled *Propos d'un Normand*. From 1906 until the start of the Great War in 1914, Alain wrote a two-page article every evening. Then, after the war—which he fought in as a soldier even though he was exempt from service and could have served as an officer—he resumed the practice of writing *propos*. All said and done, Alain produced nearly 5,000 of these little articles.

Turning philosophy into literature or journalism can be difficult for philosophers. Writing for a philosophical audience is very different than writing for a literary or general one. Certain assumptions that are made when writing for a philosophical audience cannot be made for a general audience. As such, the list of philosophers of note who successfully wrote for a general audience is a short one. Alain, to be sure, is on this list, if not heads it.[1]

Alain was able to bridge this gap through the technique he used to write his little articles. Every evening he would sit down with two sheets of paper in front of him. He then started to write his *propos* knowing that its last line would be at the bottom of the second page. He also committed himself to making no corrections, erasures, or changes. This allowed him to meet his publication deadline (all pieces were published the next day) and write only that which was directly relevant to the topic of the *propos*. The result was thousands of 50–60 line aphoristic compositions.

In 1928, 93 of Alain's *propos* dealing with the theme of happiness (*bonheur*) were published as *Propos sur le bonheur*, which became a best-selling book. The lines above are from the penultimate *propos* in this collection entitled 'The Obligation to be Happy'. It is dated March 16, 1923, and was entitled as to leave no doubt as to his position on happiness. It was a position steeped in practical wisdom tempered with an endless bounty of cheerfulness and cheeky irony. Alain encouraged people to not complain or burden others with their problems. Rather, even when they are confronted with extremely difficult situations, he encouraged his readers to present a happy face. For Alain, those who *choose* to be happy will be the recipients of great rewards.

As someone who experienced first-hand the horrors of the Great War and regarded war itself to be an absolute evil, Alain believed observance of his practical wisdom about happiness might have resulted in avoiding this epic catastrophe. 'For it is my opinion that all these cadavers, all these ruins and wild expenditures and precautionary offensives', wrote Alain, 'are the work of men who have never managed to be happy and who cannot abide those who *try to be*' (cited in Bruckner 2006: 243, my emphasis). The last words here are emphasised to point out that happiness is something that we need to continuously work at by vowing to ourselves that we will be happy and by teaching happiness to others including our students and children. Teaching, that is, '[n]ot the art of being happy when misfortune befalls you', writes Alain, 'that I leave to the Stoics'.[2] But rather, teaching 'the art of being happy when things are fairly good and treating moments of bitterness and regret as no more than minor troubles and small problems' (Alain cited in Bruckner 2006: 243).

Alain's aphoristic approach to happiness is aimed at a world that needs help in recovering from a great catastrophe such as the First World War of 1914–1918. There is no grand philosophical position on happiness other than practical wisdom such as monitoring your moods and getting plenty of exercise. This practical wisdom includes cures for seemingly everything:

> how to stop coughing (by swallowing to calm the irritation), how to cure yourself of the hiccups (by yawning), how to remove a gnat or a bit of grit from your eye (be sure not to rub the eye—look at the tip of your nose so that tears begin to flow, washing it out), how not to become bored in a train (by taking delight in watching

> the countryside pass by), how to speak to someone who is sick (by avoiding pity) and so on.
>
> (Bruckner 2006: 243, paraphrasing Alain)

Moreover, often packed into Alain's 'cures' for unhappiness are philosophical lessons. He views them as teaching moments brought on by thoughtful reflection on physical discomfort, or, more simply, if you will, *affect*. For example, consider his reflections on curing insomnia:

> Insomnia can teach us something here; and we are all familiar with this singular affliction which can lead us to believe that existence itself is unbearable. But we must take a closer look. Self-control is part of our existence; better, it directs and makes secure our existence. First of all, through action. The thoughts of a man who is sawing wood soon work to his own benefit. When the pack is out hunting, the dogs do not fight among themselves. Thus the first remedy for the ills of thought is to saw wood. But thought that is thoroughly awakened is in itself calming; by making a choice, it clears the air. To return to the malady of insomnia: you want to sleep, and you command yourself to refrain from moving or making a choice. In this absence of control, soon both your movements and your ideas are proceeding along a mechanical track; the dogs start fighting. Every movement is convulsive, and every thought is biting. You begin to have doubts about your best friend; all signs are interpreted unfavorably; in your own eyes, you seem ridiculous and stupid. These images are very strong, and it is not the hour to go out and saw wood.
>
> (Alain 1989: 251)

Thus, in this passage from 'One Must Vow', the final essay in *Propos sur le Bonheur*, Alain moves nimbly between proposing a cure for insomnia to contemplating our existence and the role of pessimism in it. To avoid the destructive force of pessimism, says Alain, we must 'vow to be happy'. This is because 'optimism requires an oath', whereas pessimism does not. For Alain, 'we create unhappiness quite naturally as soon as we do nothing', therefore to 'cure' this unhappiness it is *necessary* that we vow to be happy. Just as the 'master's whip must put a stop to the dogs' howling', the vow to be happy puts a stop to the fighting doubts of unhappiness (Alain 1989: 251).

Eventually, the type of happiness or well-being journalism initiated by Alain became commonplace in newspapers through regular features on relationship advice (e.g. 'Dear Abby'), health and beauty tips, self-remedies, and recreational guides. My favourite though in this mix is the daily horoscope, which is the ultimate happiness tool: 'The stars show the kind of day you'll have!' Thus, the most visible remainder of Alain's philosophical contribution is the happiness journalism that is still a feature of many daily newspapers. It is a most unlikely legacy for someone who the French regarded as a radical philosopher of comparable important to Descartes—and whose students included some of the most important French thinkers of the twentieth century.

One of them, the French biographer and novelist, André Maurois, went so far as to predict 80 years ago that in the year 2040 Alain's writings will eclipse in importance the more well-known philosophical classics from the period. Those eclipsed classics would most likely include the writings of Ferdinand de Saussure, Henri Bergson, Henri Poincaré, and Pierre Duhem, among others from the first quarter of the twentieth century. 'Some few of us realize that in a hundred years Alain's writings will be more widely appreciated than works which are today considered classics', wrote Maurois in 1940. 'I was happy recently when an American professor of philosophy said to me', continues Maurois, 'Do you know that France is the home of a great man who is comparatively unknown, an essayist who writes under the name of Alain?' 'He is far from unknown', responded Maurois. 'He is known among those who are worthy of knowing him!' (Alain 1989: v).

Maurois thought that by now we would have come to view Alain as the Montaigne of his age (Kolbert 231). He is said to have read every day and every evening a few pages of Alain's *Propos*, and for decades thought about how he would present his teacher's aphorisms and thoughts in a systematic matter (Kolbert 63). Finally, in 1950, he published an eponymous book on Alain that became a best seller. Maurois saw Alain a master essayist who taught us about the importance of willpower; about the value of the orderly, clear, and logical Cartesian method of problem solving; about the horror of superstitions, religious doctrines, and fear of the unknown; and finally, about the importance of a concise, direct, and economical style of writing (Kolbert 64).

Nevertheless, today, those who are worthy of knowing Alain are the unabashed proponents of happiness and practitioners of well-being through self-cure. Their works can be found in the myriad of relationship advice, health and beauty tips, and self-remedies that are now mainstream content for newspapers, blogs, and websites—if not also the *happiness industry*. But let's not get too far ahead of ourselves here. We will turn to the happiness industry in the next two sections. Given, as we shall see, the total domination of society by this industry, perhaps it is only a matter of time now for Maurois's prediction to come to pass. That is, for Alain to be widely recognised and read as *the* philosopher who paved the way for curing unhappiness in the new millennium. To date though, he is still a relatively obscure theorist of happiness.[3]

Clap along

'Clap along', sings Pharrell Williams, 'if you feel like happiness is the truth'. And people in the United States and around the world did—in record numbers. Released in June of 2013, Pharrell's 'Happy' was the best-selling song in the United States in 2014 with 6.45 million copies sold. In the United Kingdom, it sold more than 1.6 million copies in 2014 making it the most downloaded track *ever* in the United Kingdom beating out Robin Thicke's 'Blurred Lines' and Adele's 'Someone Like You', which, respectively, sold 1.59 and 1.53 million copies each (Szalai 2014). In the first quarter of 2014 'Happy' was streamed a mind-boggling 43 million times on Pandora. Still, these streams only resulted in $2,700 in publisher and songwriter royalties, which did not sit well with Pharrell and led him to join a group of artists demanding that YouTube take down thousands of songs it did not have permission to use (Kosoff n.d.). In the case of 'Happy', the song was used frequently on YouTube as background music to international expressions of 'happiness'.

Literally, thousands of videos can be found on YouTube of people from around the world dancing to Pharrell's hit song. In fact, by May of 2014, there were more than 1,500 videos including an independently launched website (wearehappyfrom.com) to showcase them. For example, there is a video of folks in the High Tatras Mountains in Slovakia swinging to his song against a breathtaking landscape that has been viewed 7.3 million times since it was posted in March of 2014 (Tatranec Tatranský 2014). There is also a video from Australia of shots of 'happy' dogs and cats posted in May of 2014 that had 14.3 million views, double that of the High Tatras video, perhaps implying that the happiness of our animal friends is just as 'true' worldwide as that of their human keepers (Catmantoo 2014). Then, of course, there is the YouTube video of the Minions dancing to Pharrell's international hit. Posted in June of 2013, the Minions 'Happy' video has been viewed 76.7 million times (#Trailer 2013). Still, the viewership of these 'Happy' videos pales next to the number of views of the Official Music Video of 'Happy' by Pharrell Williams. Posted on November 21, 2013, it has now been viewed over *one billion times*—1,081,323,789 times to be exact (iamOTHER 2013).

To say that this song has been wildly popular worldwide is substantiated by both its sales figures and the many videos done by people wanting to share with others expressions of their happiness. But, as we will see in the next section, this song is just a small piece of a much larger industry centred on the development, promotion, and sale of 'happiness' as a product. It is an industry connected to among other things a new branch of psychology, the rise of big data, and the military industrial complex. The exponential rise and growth of the happiness industry both are fuelled by and fuels the blissful belief so directly put in Pharrell's song that 'happiness *is* the truth'.

In just the few examples from YouTube noted above, all are used to sell products: the Slovaks want us to vacation in the High Tatras Mountains so use a thumbnail view of a woman in a bikini to get viewers to successfully click what is essentially a tourism video; the Australian video, while foregoing bikinis, uses an even more effective clickbait tool, the dog and cat video, to lure viewers into what is essentially a promotional video for an 'off leash training program' for dogs which offers a 'doggy outing service', wherein up to a dozen dogs are picked up by the dog trainer and taken to a dog friendly place to play and practice their training, and are then taken home after getting a rinse and a nail trim, if needed; the Minions video of 'Happy' was used to promote the film, *Despicable Me 2* (2013), for which the song was originally written before it eventually landed on Pharrell's 2014 album G I R L. Apparently, though, it took him a long time to reach an agreement with the film studio about the song.

'My song submissions for this scene [in *Despicable Me 2*] were rejected nine times', says Pharrell in a New York Times op-ed. Of this long process to produce a hit song for a 76-million-dollar film that grossed 970 million dollars worldwide, one critic writes, 'Looks like we could have lived in a world where "Happy" did not exist'—or at least was not as profitable (Rettig 2014).

But in spite of the overwhelming international response to Pharrell's song, which at less than four minutes in length manages to sing the word 'happy' almost 60 times, some people were not so happy with 'Happy'. A YouTube video from May of 2014 set to 'Happy' by some Iranian fans led to their arrest. The police chief said the song represented public vulgarity and also hurt public chastity. The president of Iran, Hassan Rouhani, criticised the arrest in a May 21, 2014 tweet saying '#Happiness is our people's right. We shouldn't be too hard on behaviors caused by joy' (Rouhani 2014). Though the director and the dancers were later released (Mackey 2014), they each received a suspended punishment of 91 lashes. This means that if within a period of three years they commit *another* crime then their lashing will be carried out (Dehghan 2014).

But maybe Alain *still* has something to teach us about happiness—and maybe it is not found in the story of Pharrell's corporate music experience but comes from one of the greatest bands in the world—the Rolling Stones. Compare Pharrell's experience of writing 'Happy' to Keith Richard's account of writing a song of the same title for the Rolling Stones album *Exile on Main Street* (1972a). 'We did ["Happy" (1972b)] in an afternoon', writes Richards in his autobiography, *Life* (2010):

> [I]n only four hours, cut and done. At four o'clock it was on tape. It was no Rolling Stones record. It's got the name on it, but it was actually Jimmy Miller on drums, Bobby Keys on baritone and that was basically it. And then I overdubbed bass and guitar. We were just waiting for everybody to turn up for the real sessions for the rest of the night and we thought, we're here; let's see if we can come up with something. I'd written it that day.
>
> (Richards 2010: 308)

The words to the song 'just came tripping off the tongue', says Richards. While a hit for the Rolling Stones, it was written much like Alain's *propos*. If happiness *is* for sale, then the commodity that Keith Richards exiled on Main Street is very different from the one corporately produced by Pharrell.

Alain, as we saw, did not believe that happiness was a commodity. In fact, based upon the way he wrote about it, as grounded in a kind of philosophical self-examination elicited by physical discomfort or affect, a path to its commodification seems remote at best. But perhaps, like Socrates who refused to take money for his philosophical lessons with full knowledge of others (the Sophists) who did, Alain wanted to promote a version of happiness that was *not* a commodity in a world where it was fast becoming one. And it should not have been difficult for Alain to envision the commodification of happiness given that his daily *propos* on happiness sold a lot of newspapers in France. For Alain, selling happiness came down to convincing the public that it was possible to be happy in a world ravaged by a catastrophic war and financial despair. Happiness *needed to be* something that could not be purchased because people just did not have the means to acquire it if it came with a financial cost.

A century later, however, happiness is selling better than ever. Pharrell's 'Happy' peaked at Number 1 in the music charts of 19 countries.

So too are philosophers who write about happiness and attempt to deepen our understanding of the pursuit of happiness. Take, for example, Slavoj Žižek. One of his YouTube lectures on happiness takes two minutes and has been viewed 1.6 million times (Žižek 2012), and his two and a half hour debate with Jordan Peterson on happiness in capitalism versus Marxism has been viewed 145,000 times (Žižek and Peterson 2019). In spite of, as we will see later, their differences regarding the pursuit of happiness, Alain the '*vulgarisateur*' (Wellek 1992: 23) would have been pleased to see this very public philosopher bring the topic of happiness into the wider arena that the Internet now affords intrepid thinkers and industrious writers.

It bears mentioning that part of the widespread appeal of Žižek's philosophy is his willingness to both take popular culture seriously and to use popular media such as YouTube to share it with others. While I have no doubt that Žižek would be interested in discussing Pharrell's 'Happy' through the lens of his particular version of Hegelian Marxism, one grounded in the psychoanalysis of Lacan (which we will turn to in the next chapter), I also have no doubt that his Marxist predecessors from the Frankfurt School, such as Max Horkheimer, Theodor Adorno, and Herbert Marcuse would have *no* interest in examining happiness through the lens of their Freudian version of Hegelian Marxism. To foreground this point, consider Žižek's anecdote regarding an encounter between Fredric Jameson and Marcuse: when Jameson was a student of Marcuse's in San Diego, he brought his professor a Rolling Stones album as a gift. Marcuse's response, says Žižek via Jameson: 'Total aggressive dismissal; he despised it' (Rasmussen 2004).

One imagines a similar response from Horkheimer and Adorno if presented with a Stones album. As for a popular song written *for* a movie, one imagines an even more extreme response (if that is possible) from the duo that argues that movies are not art, but rather commodities produced by the culture industry. 'Film, radio, and magazines make up a system which is uniform as a whole and in every part', write Horkheimer and Adorno in *Dialectic of Enlightenment* (Horkheimer and Adorno 1972: 120). This system is subservient to the 'absolute power of capitalism' (Horkheimer and Adorno 1972: 120). The interests of the motion picture, broadcasting, and publishing industries are 'economically interwoven' (Horkheimer and Adorno 1972: 123) with other, more powerful, capitalist industries such as the banking, petroleum, utility, and chemical industries. The culture industry produces homogeneous and monotonous commodities replete with interchangeable details and ready-made clichés. For them, the homogeneity of art produced by the culture industry serves an important social and political function: it maintains the status quo and destroys individuality. This mass art aims to produce, control, and discipline its consumers. It also aims to deprive them of amusement by stunting their 'powers of imagination and spontaneity' (Horkheimer and Adorno 1972: 126). 'The culture industry does not sublimate; it represses' the desire for happiness, argue Horkheimer and Adorno, making 'laughter the instrument of the fraud practiced on happiness' (Horkheimer and Adorno 1972: 140).

We'll turn to some of these frauds practiced on happiness in the next chapter, but for now, let's stay tuned to all of those people around the world dancing, singing, and clapping that happiness is the truth. Based on the response to Pharrell's song, the pursuit of happiness is regarded as a self-evident truth by many people the world over including the president of a country where some of its citizens were imprisoned for posting a video that utilises the song. Still, in spite of the international renown of happy hit records such as Pharrell's, the music industry is just one component of a much larger one dedicated to the production and consumption of happiness. Selling happiness, as we will see in the next section, is a big business today—perhaps the biggest business of them all.

Big happiness

To be sure, happiness today *is* a commodity—and it may very well be the best-selling product on Amazon. The free market rewards consumer demand with more products. The axioms of neoliberalism dictate that *everything* is for sale and that everything can—and should be—plundered for profit including happiness. Given this, it should not be surprising to learn that happiness inquiry has for several centuries been extended from philosophy, its traditional domain, to several branches of science in addition to most recently, the military, industry, and business.

If John Locke, as we shall see later, brought the pursuit of happiness into government in the late seventeenth century, then Jeremy Bentham made it the *business* of government in the late eighteenth century:

> The business of government is to promote the happiness of the society, by punishing and rewarding. That part of its business which consists in punishing, is more particularly the subject of penal law. In proportion as an act tends to disturb that happiness, in proportion as the tendency of it is pernicious, will be the demand

> it creates for punishment. What happiness consists of we have already seen: enjoyment of pleasures, security from pains.
>
> (Bentham 1879: 70)

Moreover, ever since Bentham speculated on happiness as a *measurable* physical occurrence within the human body, science has slowly been working towards a quantitative means of measuring human sensation in a quest towards greater control over the pursuit of happiness. Bentham, while speculating that the choices for measuring utility might come down to pulse rate or money, did not even come close to imagining the sciences and industries that would develop around sensation as a means to advancing the pursuit of happiness. The work of neuroscience stands out here as a locus of activity. It has, for example, located areas in the brain that produce positive and negative emotions, and has even offered neural explanations as to why singing improves our well-being.

Still, it would not be until the mid-nineteenth century before there was a systematic attempt to construct a quantitative measure of sensation. The major figure here was the German experimental psychologist, philosopher, and physicist, Gustav Theodor Fechner, who founded psychophysics, which, in turn, inspired a number of twentieth-century scientists and philosophers. Fechner's psychophysics argued that mind and matter, though separate entities, have a stable, mathematical relationship to each other. This numerical ratio between mind and world led therapists, analysts, and psychiatrists that followed in Fechner's footsteps to refocus their attention from the object that caused subjects to have feelings to the subject having these feelings.

Also in the mid-nineteenth century, there was an effort to connect sensations produced via the nervous system with money. The English psychologist William Stanley Jevons established that economics could no longer ignore psychology. He explored economics as the science of pleasure and pain, and following Bentham, regarded the mind as a kind of calculator. Nevertheless, by the 1930s, economics was once again disconnected from psychology through the theory of preferences developed by Alfred Marshall and Vilfredo Pareto.

As the pursuit of happiness drifts away from its philosophical foundations and flirts with psychological and economic ones, its ties to business gradually grow stronger, particularly in the United States, where the histories of psychology and consumerism become intertwined in the twentieth century. It has been argued that American psychology has no philosophical heritage but was rather was born out of the world of big business (Davies 2015: 85).

Psychology in America was co-opted in the early twentieth century by business interests eager for findings that could be used to better determine and control consumer behaviour. Key to this co-optation was the behavioural psychology of John B. Watson (see especially Watson 1913, 1925), which soon became the property of the Madison Avenue advertising industry. In 1920, Watson joined J. Walter Thompson, a large Madison Avenue advertising firm, at 'a salary four times what he was earning at Johns Hopkins' (Davies 2015: 94). By this time, the advertising industry, excited by the potential of using psychology to increase its effectiveness, was willing to pay intellectuals to work on behalf of business. Even Adorno was pulled into this orbit by working on a study for CBS of its radio audiences (Davies 2015: 99). Moreover, in addition to the birth of advertising science based on the psychology of happiness, there was also a growing demand among managers and policymakers for a science of workplace happiness. And it was here, argues William Davies, that the happiness industry was officially born:

> For Bentham, happiness was something which resulted from certain activities and choices. Neo-classical economists such as Jevons and behaviourist psychologists such as Watson assumed something similar, implying that individuals could be lured to make certain choices by dangling a pleasurable carrot in front of them. But in the context of business consultancy and individual coaching, happiness looks altogether different. Suddenly, it is represented as an input to certain strategies and projects, a resource to be drawn upon, which will yield more money in return. Bentham and Jevons's psychological premise, that money yields a proportionate quantity of happiness, is spun on its head, suggesting instead that a quantity of happiness will yield a certain amount of money.
>
> (Davies 2015: 114)

Symptomatic of this reversal, Davies cites neuroscientist Paul Zak, who suggests that we view happiness like a muscle that requires regular exercising in order to keep it strong and healthy (Davies 2015: 114). Apropos, albeit satirically, the citizens of Huxley's *Brave New World* who live under a government of happiness, grow 'stronger' by frequently flexing this muscle—many times even under the influence of *soma*, a drug designed to keep the happiness muscle strong.

Flash-forward now a century from the birth of happiness in the service of workplace science and the advertising industry to the era of neoliberalism where reverence for the management of happiness is coupled with extreme individualism and competiveness. American psychiatry is now completely cut out of the happiness industry to the point where 80% of the prescriptions for antidepressant drugs in the United States are written not by psychiatrists, but rather by medical doctors and primary care practitioners. Moreover, the use of anti-depressant drugs such as Prozac has reached epidemic proportions. American psychiatry became a partner in this crisis when in 1980 the *Diagnostic and Statistical Manual of Mental Disorders* (DSM) jumped from 180 categories (DSM-II) to 292 categories (DSM-III) almost overnight. Moreover, DSM-III reduced the diagnostic symptom time from one month to two weeks, and now allowed for mental illness diagnosis to be determinable solely by observation and classification without any corresponding explanation as to why it had arisen (Davies 2015: 174–175). In short, from the perspective of American psychiatry, mental health and happiness have been sold out to the big drug industries.

Moreover, contributing to this situation is the growth of 'positive psychology' and 'happiness studies', two fields that 'helped shift the focus among researchers and a broader public from mental illness to emotional well-being' (Horowitz 2018: 1). Whereas the roots of the shift from an emphasis on mental health to personal well-being can be traced back to the late 1930s and can be found flourishing today in the influential and growing fields of positive psychology and happiness studies, Martin Seligman's 1998 presidential address to the American Psychological Association (APA) is the widely accepted story of the origin of positive psychology (Horowitz 2018: 15–18). It was at this APA meeting that Seligman called on professional psychologists to emphasise well-being instead of mental illness. In specific, Seligman encouraged his colleagues 'to shift the focus in psychology from illness, misery, and pessimism to well-being, happiness, and optimism' (Horowitz 2018: 18).

Horowitz, the foremost historian of positive psychology, has pointed out that the optimistic world view of positive psychology developed 'during a time that saw a worldwide refugee crisis, the spread of religiously and ethnically based violence, and the anger that arose from the adverse consequences of globalization and technological changes' (Horowitz 2018: 2). Moreover, through the work of excellent marketing, the specialised knowledge of the discipline of psychology was 'transferred into the public domain' by positive psychology and transformed 'into salable products' (Horowitz 2018: 2). 'Literary agents and publishers played key roles in making it possible for professors to crash through the boundaries around the universities and take over public discussions', writes Horowitz. 'Broad audiences could be easily reached because experts [in positive psychology] gave the obvious—sleep more, have close friends, engage in work—a scientific basis' (Horowitz 2018: 2). Consequently, happiness via positive psychology has become a 'big business' wherein 'tens of millions of people and organizations spend billions of dollars in an effort to increase subjective well-being' (Horowitz 2018: 239). These products include but are not limited to how-to books, payments to therapists, purchase of drugs, workshop attendance, funding from government and private agencies, apps, TED talks, web sites, positive psychology coaching, and corporate and school consultants (Horowitz 2018: 239–281).

Interestingly though, while many positive psychologists acknowledged the importance of the philosophical contributions of Aristotle, Bentham, Charles Darwin, and William James on their understanding of happiness and well-being, they tended to shy away from the American tradition of positive thinking, one that Horowitz views as reaching a high point in the mid-twentieth century with Norman Vincent Peale's *The Power of Positive Thinking* (1952), which to date has sold more than five million copies worldwide, and stretching back at least as far as the work of Mary Baker Eddy, the founder of The Church of Christ the Scientist in the last quarter of the nineteenth century.

One of the major hawkers of the products of positive psychology has been Oprah Winfrey, who saw herself on a mission with 'the message: Make yourself happy' (Horowitz 2018: 247). She has been widely regarded as one of America's most influential promoters of positivity and happiness. The Oprah Winfrey Show (1986–2011) reached audiences in over 100 countries and in the United States alone reached 50 million viewers. This is important to consider because it speaks to the international reach of her book club, which started in 1996. For many of her viewers, the books she covered over the years 1996–2011—70 in total—became required reading. In 2012, her book club went online and continues to offer book reviews and reading lists. Given her championing of positive psychology, one might consider her book club efforts in view of her position on happiness—a position that continues to exert an extraordinary power to alter the repute and sales of literature with regard to considerations of well-being.

Still, in spite of the popularity today of positive psychology through Oprah's show and other mainstream venues such as TED talks, it has been contested both within and outside of the field. From questions regarding the relationship between higher income and the enhancement of well-being and the relevance of the field to public policy, to the very meaning of happiness and well-being, many of the major conclusions of the field have been 'challenged, modified, or even abandoned' (Horowitz 2018: 4). Moreover, because the rise of positive psychology is linked to the development of market-based neoliberalism, the critique of the latter is often transferred as well to the former. Horowitz finds it therefore 'ironic that positive psychology came to be promoted by marketing, even as many of its practitioners minimized the benefits of higher incomes or unbridled immersion in materialistic culture, while others offered a gospel based on prosperity' (Horowitz 2018: 5).

Though both positive psychology and happiness studies developed separately mid-twentieth century, they would later merge to the point that it has become very difficult for most to distinguish them from each other. To make this easier, positive psychology might be regarded as focusing on the improvement of the individual, whereas happiness studies looks towards improving society. In particular, whereas positive psychology focuses on 'positive mental health, meaning, and eudaimonia', happiness studies concentrate on 'subjective well-being, life satisfaction, and a broadly defined hedonic happiness' (Horowitz 2018: 2). Also, whereas happiness studies are concerned with income inequality, environmentalism, social class, and gender, positive psychology centres on issues of character. Finally, as each relies on 'data', each should both be regarded as additional chapters in the 'science' of happiness.

It might also be noted that the interweaving of the 'science' of happiness with social media innovation in the age of neoliberalism has created its own set of problems. For example, it has been shown that the social media technology such as Facebook actually makes people feel *worse* about their lives rather than better. Still, people continue to turn to social media in pursuit of happiness—as is evidenced by all those YouTube videos made by people dancing to Pharrell's 'Happy'. The question is, did all of these social media expressions of 'happiness' actually make people feel better or worse about their lives? These of course are the type of questions that positive psychology and happiness studies are highly motivated to answer, particularly if provided with the right set of data. Why? Because the aim of positive psychology and happiness studies is to *improve* our happiness and well-being. Hence, if it can be determined that viewing social-media expressions of 'happiness' contributes to our happiness, then such viewing will be encouraged. Otherwise, it must be avoided lest it place our well-being in jeopardy.

Fortunately, for these fields (but maybe not for our privacy), there has been an explosion of happiness and wellness data that is clearly an effect of forms of surveillance that can be traced back to Bentham's panopticon. Though these forms of surveillance were only philosophical speculation in Bentham in support of the government business of happiness, new technologies of the late twentieth and early twenty-first centuries have brought them to dystopian fruition.

In an episode of the series, Black Mirror, for example, a child is implanted with a device which has the ability to block by distortion 'disturbing' images and sounds the child perceives. Throughout the episode, we see the effects of this technology on both child and parent. Control society and big data meet the pursuit of happiness in this episode as the device allows parents to both continuously monitor and record their child's behaviour as well as filter its content. A small implant is painlessly put into the child's head. It allows the parent to: (1) Monitor Location—if the child goes missing, the parent just needs to enter a PIN and law enforcement will automatically be notified; (2) Monitor Vitals—this feature gives parents the ability to monitor their children's blood health, electrolytes, cholesterol, red and white blood cell count, ipids, heart rate, iron level, tryglycerites, and glucose—and to remediate immediately vital health problems; and (3) Monitor Perception—the device allows parents to see what the child is seeing with the added option of parental controls that place a filter over stressful things that the child sees or hears. All of the data including a complete catalogue of the child's perceptions is stored and accessible by the parent at any time. In short, big data and surveillance technology allows for the scientific control of human happiness (Black Mirror 2017).

But what makes this episode even scarier is that there are already on the market many devices with the ability to monitor the behaviour and, especially for followers of the behaviourist psychology of Watson, the *happiness* of children. Mimo Baby, for example, is a 'onesie [that] allows parents to monitor a newborn's activity and temperature via smart phone'; Arlo Baby, an 'internet-connected camera which features alerts for movement and crying'; FiLIP is a 'a wearable platform that allows parents to track their child's location, calls, and texts'; Circle is 'a smart router that lets parents limit screen time and filter the content children access'; Fitbit Ace is a 'smart activity tracker which tracks a child's every move'; TeenSafe 'gives parents access to a child's call history, transcripts of their text messages, and their web-browsing history'; and MotoSafety 'provides real-time feedback for parents on their child's driving habits, daily report cards, and arrival alerts' (McHendry 2019: 206).

The rise of *big* data in pursuit of happiness then is different from the data *survey*. The latter was collected with the intention of analysing it, whereas with the former this is not. The dream of data science is that eventually the separate disciplines of psychology, economics, sociology, and management will eventually be melted down into one general science of choice. Thus, because according to behavioural psychology happiness is determinable by choice, this general science of choice is ultimately a general science of happiness. For some, this also signals the end of theory, namely, the end of parallel disciplines such as philosophy, psychology, sociology, and economics working in consort to explain and solve common problems. If neuroscience and big data analytics can be synthesised into a hard set of laws of decision-making, and behavioural surveillance continues to improve and become more commonplace, predicting what makes humans happy may become a hard science. And just as Amazon through big data analysis now comes pretty close to knowing your exact purchasing behaviour with its 'predicative shopping' features, so too will the combination of neuroscience and big data through 'predictive happiness' know what brings you pleasure and what causes you misery. Once this is determined, we are no longer pursuing happiness, but rather will be *pursued by* happiness.

Big happiness is the domain where the pursuit of happiness and the pursuit of the market become two sides of the same coin through big data and control society. Welcome to the *brave new world* of Huxley—a world he fictionalised almost a century ago and lived long enough to regard as becoming increasingly and horrifically similar to the real one. And few today would disagree with his assessment. Let's now take a closer look at the role, cost, and conditions of happiness in Huxley's *Brave New World*, and the way psychology was used to posit it.

Brave happy world

When 'Our Ford', the Resident Controller of Western Europe, Mustapha Mond, spoke of psychological matters, 'for some inscrutable reason, he chose to call himself "Our Freud"' (Huxley 2006: 39), writes Huxley in *Brave New World*. While the reason may be enigmatic to the narrator of *Brave New World*, it is quite clear to the reader: to identify one of the major sources of this dystopic future society, psychology. Continues Huxley,

> Our Freud had been the first to reveal the appalling dangers of family life. The world was full of fathers—was therefore full of misery; full of mothers—therefore of every kind of perversion from sadism to chastity; full of brothers, sisters, uncles, aunts—full of madness and suicide.
>
> (Huxley 2006: 39)

The 'brave new world' of Huxley's dystopic satire is a 'World State' set 600 years in the future (A[fter]. F[ord]. 632) that is controlled by a group of ten of these Fords (or Freuds). The sway between Our Ford and Our Freud is one between the two major world-making axes of the future: the industrialised world exemplified by the development of the assembly line technique of mass production, homogenisation, and consumption of disposable goods (Ford) and the psychological world exemplified by the development of techniques of psychological manipulation, classical conditioning, and sleep-learning (Freud).

It must be remembered too that in the summer of 1931, when Huxley was composing this novel, both Henry Ford *and* Sigmund Freud were not historical figures, but both very much living people. The American industrialist and founder of Ford Motor Company was 68 and would live until 1947, and the father of psychoanalysis was 75 and would live until 1939. So too was H. G. Wells, whose utopian novels, particularly *A Modern Utopia* (1905) and *Men Like Gods* (1923), were some of the direct objects of Huxley's satire. In a letter that summer to Mrs. Kethevan Roberts, Huxley said

> I am writing a novel about the future—on the horror of the Wellsian Utopia and a revolt against it. Very difficult. I have hardly enough imagination to deal with such a subject. But it is none the less interesting work.
>
> (Huxley 1969: 348)

Though not one of the rulers of the world state, Wells appears in Huxley's novel simply as 'Mr. Wells'. Fittingly, this British writer and utopian socialist published *The Work, Wealth, and Happiness of Mankind* the same year that Huxley was working on his satire of the pursuit of happiness. Wells, who died in 1946, was 65 when Huxley was writing *Brave New World*, was not pleased with the novel (Huxley 1969: 358–359). He accused Huxley of 'treason to science and defeatist pessimism' (Sawyer 2002: 84). Finally, though not a figure in Huxley's novel, it might be added that Alain's best-selling book on happiness, *Propos sur le Bonheur*, came out only a few years before the publication of *Brave New World*. Moreover, Alain too was 63 when the Huxley novel was being written and would live until 1951.

In short, the object of Huxley's satire were some of the major figures and theories of the early twentieth-century, whose major practitioners were all living at the time of its composition. What made this satire different though from the previous four that he wrote—*Crome Yellow* (1921), *Antic Hay* (1923), *Those Barren Leaves* (1925), and *Point Counterpoint* (1928)—was that *Brave New World* was a dystopia. Whereas satire aims to ridicule or rebuke someone or something through a mix of ironic humour and criticism, dystopia goes one step further by imagining a world, often in the future, where these ridiculed or rebuked ideas or theories are put into practice and demonstrably lead to catastrophic consequences for society. If satire is more about jest, then dystopia is more about matters of life and death—and catastrophe. This needs to be pointed out because Huxley is not merely poking fun at the ideas of Ford, Freud, and Wells, but saying that they will lead to catastrophe. In the case of Wells, this is a particularly brutal assessment because at least since the publication of *The Outline of History* in 1919, his ostensive goal was to help the world *avoid* catastrophe through education and the formation of the World State. This negative assessment of Wells is only amplified further in Chapter 4 when Badiou applies the term 'evil' to 'catastrophes' of happiness.

Of the novel itself, the general plot is a fairly common one in science fiction. An individual rises up against a dystopic future world in an assertion of freedom and individuality. However, what sets *Brave New World* apart from similarly plotted novels is its treatment of happiness in relation to the axes of Fordism and psychology. These axes meet in the 'civilisation' of a world of mass-produced happiness. In this world, citizens are produced in artificial wombs in a Fordist assembly-line technique. Conditioning is used in childhood to indoctrinate citizens into a class-hierarchy based on intelligence and required-labour task. 'All conditioning aims at … making people like their unescapable social destiny', says the Director of Hatcheries and Conditioning. This is the '*secret* of happiness and virtue', that is, 'liking what you've got to do' (Huxley 2006: 16, my emphasis). But there is an even darker secret to happiness 'hidden' in Huxley's novel—one that ties it to his thoughts at the time on intelligence, eugenics, and politics.

This 'hidden' Huxley, who is an elitist technocrat and eugenicist influenced by Wells and H. L. Mencken, is 'revealed' most directly by David Bradshaw in his 1994 edited volume, *The Hidden Huxley: Contempt and Compassion for the Masses 1920–36*. This early (hidden) Huxley is very different from the pacifist, spiritualist, and humanist one of later years. During the late 1920 and early 1930s, Huxley published several essays defending 'eugenic policies of encouraging higher birthrates among the "intellectual classes" and sterilising the lower-class "unfit", which he believed would improve the inherited mental abilities of future generations and lead to responsible citizenship'

(Woiak 2007: 106). Moreover, during this period, 'eugenics was not a nightmare prospect' for Huxley, 'but rather the best hope for designing a better world if used in the right ways by the right people' (Woiak 2007: 106). He maintained that 'human life would be improved by increasing the innate intellectual abilities of the population' (Woiak 2007: 106). Writes Huxley shortly after the publication of *Brave New World*,

> About 99.5% of the entire population of the planet are as stupid and philistine ... as the great masses of the English. The important thing, it seems to me, is not to attack the 99.5% ... but to try to see that the 0.05% survives, keeps its quality up to the highest possible level, and, if possible, dominates the rest. The imbecility of the 99.5% is appalling—but after all, what else can you expect?
>
> (Huxley 1933 cited by Bradshaw 1994: xx)

These and other 'hidden' thoughts by Huxley on intelligence, eugenics, and politics complicate his satire, adding to it 'a prediction of biological advances, a commentary on the social roles of science and scientists, and a plan for reforming society' (Woiak 2007: 106). To say the least, these darker 'secrets' add an extremely unsavoury dimension to his thoughts on happiness.

Essays by Huxley from this period had titles such as 'Are We Growing Stupider? [1932]' (Huxley 2001a) and 'What is Happening to Our Population? [1934]' (Huxley 1994). The eugenics that he championed though was a mainstream line in Britain and the United States that focused on the problem of 'feeblemindedness' (Woiak 2007: 109), wherein low IQ was viewed as a threat to society and a source of social ills. Moreover, in both countries, 'a strict division between the socio-economic classes in terms of mental and moral qualities' was assumed—a division which Huxley exaggerated in his novel through 'superior' Alphas and 'impaired' Epsilons (Woiak 2007: 109). Still, it needs to be pointed out that the eugenics movement was so diverse and complex in the early twentieth-century that most readers of the novel today are not likely to see its class division as an expression of Anglo-American eugenic concerns and policies, which today are often only associated with Nazi racial eugenics (Woiak 2007: 110).[4]

However, when one does recognise the eugenics movement in Huxley's novel its compulsory genetic manipulation and meritocratic rule appear less as satire and more as authentic proposals for social and political organisation after the demise of democracy. A few years before writing the novel, Huxley says

> How do they expect democratic institutions to survive in a country where an increasing percentage of the population are mentally defective? Half-wits fairly ask for dictators. Improve the average intelligence of the population and self-governance will become, not only inevitable, but efficient.
>
> (Huxley 2001b: 187)

During this period, Huxley also rejects the Enlightenment idea of the equality of man (Huxley 1928: 23–55) and that everyone is 'equally endowed with moral worth and intellectual ability' (Huxley 2001b: 187). In addition, he proposes that IQ tests ought to be utilised for the purposes of who should run for office or vote (Huxley 1928: 56–120 and 195–204). Here, the satire of a society run by Alphas and supported by the menial labourers, the Episolons, represents his worst fears at the time about both the end of democracy and biological decay. 'The ideal state', wrote Huxley at the time, 'is one in which there is a material democracy controlled by an aristocracy of the intellect' (Huxley 2001b: 191). This ideal is very similar to the one offered by Wells in *Men Like Gods* (1923), a book that was noted earlier as the object of satire, but viewed from perspective of the 'hidden Huxley', that is, the elitist technocrat and eugenicist, it actually echoes the social and political ideals of the author at the time.

Everyone in the society of *Brave New World* is happy because through social engineering and psychological conditioning a completely stable and predictable world has been created and is maintained by a technocratic elite. This is reflected in the motto of the World State—'Community, Identity, Stability' (Huxley 2006: 3). Or, as Mustapha Mond—a character modelled after Alfred Mond, an industrialist admired by Huxley, who in 1926 amalgamated and rationalised the major British chemical companies—says, 'We believe in happiness and stability' (Huxley 2006: 222). After the revolt in the hospital, John and Bernard are called to a meeting with 'His Fordship', Mustapha Mond. It is in this meeting that Huxley lays bare the full nature of his critique of happiness through the voice of the Controller. In the meeting, the Controller reveals to them that he like John is familiar with the writings of Shakespeare and even finds them to be beautiful. However, the World State, Huxley's government of happiness, has no use for 'beautiful' 'old things' like the works of Shakespeare. 'Beauty's attractive', says Mustapha, 'and we don't want people attracted by old things' (Huxley 2006: 219). 'We want them to like new ones' (Huxley 2006: 219). The reason for this is that the new things promote social stability, whereas the old things, like the works of Shakespeare, are premised upon *social instability*. Thus, even though Shakespeare is *better* than the art produced in the World State, rejecting it is 'the price we have to pay for stability' (Huxley 2006: 220). 'You've got to choose between happiness and what people used to call high art', says the Controller. 'We've sacrificed the high art' as the price of social stability and happiness (Huxley 2006: 220).

But in sacrificing high art for happiness, the stable World State has taken something away from the resultant happiness. 'Actual happiness always looks pretty squalid in comparison with the overcompensations for misery', says the Mustapha (Huxley 2006: 221). Instability is more 'spectacular' than stability. Moreover, the contentment that comes with a stable world and happiness 'has none of the glamour of a good fight against misfortune, none of the picturesqueness of a struggle with temptation, or a fatal overthrow by passion or doubt'. Thus, concludes Mustapha, real or actual happiness is 'never grand' (Huxley 2006: 221).

Yet art is not the only enemy of real happiness. So too is science. 'Every discovery in pure science is potentially subversive; even science must sometimes be treated as possible enemy' of happiness, says Mustapha (Huxley 2006: 225). The science that underlies the World State is 'just a cookery book, with an orthodox theory of cooking that nobody's allowed to question, and a list of recipes that mustn't be added to except by special permission of the head cook', namely, the Controller (Huxley 2006: 225). Thus, for the general happiness of the World State, all of those people who have independent ideas in science and other areas, and who aim to defy orthodoxy, are sent to live together in communities isolated from the broader society. 'Happiness is a hard master', says the controller, 'particularly other people's happiness'. 'A much harder master', concedes the controller, 'if one isn't conditioned to accept it unquestioningly, than truth' (Huxley 2006: 227).

Finally, the Controller initiates the separation of happiness from truth by reference to the influence of Ford:

> Our Ford himself did a great deal to shift the emphasis from truth and beauty to comfort and happiness. Mass production demanded the shift. Universal happiness keeps the wheels steadily turning; truth and beauty can't. And, of course, whenever the masses seized political power, then it was happiness rather than truth and beauty that mattered.
>
> (Huxley 2006: 228)

The separation of happiness from truth was finalised though 'after the Nine Year's War' (Huxley 2006: 228). 'What's the point of truth or beauty or knowledge when the anthrax bombs are popping all around you?', asks the Controller. The people were ready to be controlled after this war. This control was not good for truth in the World State. 'But it's been very good for happiness. One can't have something for nothing. Happiness *has got to be paid for*' (Huxley 2006: 228, my emphasis). In sum, few novels sell happiness and, at the same time, question its price better than *Brave New World*.

Conclusion

Twenty-seven years after the writing of *Brave New World*—and the waning of his infatuation with the eugenics movement and antidemocratic politics—Huxley had the opportunity to reflect back on the novel.[5] He says that when he was writing the novel in 1931, he 'was convinced that there was still plenty of time' to avoid the 'completely organized society, the scientific caste system, the abolition of free will by methodological conditioning, the servitude made acceptable by regular doses of chemically induced happiness, the orthodoxies drummed in nightly by sleep-teaching' (Huxley 1965: 3). But in 1958, his optimism had faded. *Brave New World Revisited* catalogues his concerns regarding over-population, over-organisation, political propaganda, the arts of selling, brainwashing (i.e. the process of pressuring someone into adopting radically different beliefs by using systemic and many times forcible methods), chemical persuasion, subconscious persuasion, and hypnopaedia (i.e. learning by hearing while asleep or under hypnosis). Moreover, 'higher education is not necessarily a guarantee of higher virtue, or political wisdom' (Huxley 1965: 28). 'Under favorable conditions', writes Huxley, 'practically everybody can be converted to practically anything' (Huxley 1965: 63).

But today, rather than fight against a world where 'happiness [is] the Sovereign Good' and the 'purpose of life [is] the maintenance of well-being' (Huxley 2006: 177), many have conceded that we now live in the future that Huxley predicted—and, borrowing from Jean-Paul Sartre, there is 'no exit'. In a review of a television series based on the novel that premiered in the summer of 2020 (Huxley 2020), the reviewer announces that the series 'arrives in the future it predicted' (Soloski 2020). The challenge now for artistic representations of the novel, writes this New York Times reviewer, is 'How do you take a nearly 90-year-old novel, a literary crystal ball so dead-on that many of its predictions (chemical birth control, mood stabilisers, genetic engineering) have already come true, and still make it feel like the future' (Soloski 2020)? The showrunner, David Weiner concedes the challenge too of adapting a novel where the future is now, one in which 'Huxley was very afraid of a world in which people would become so sexually stimulated, so pharmacologically numb and so distracted by entertainment and media, that they would fail to look within and beyond themselves in uncomfortable ways' (Soloski 2020).

While the series struggles to solve the problem of a futuristic setting, it does correct some of its 'ugly flares of racism and misogyny' by 'pivoting toward equality, race-bending and gender-flipping several of the supporting characters' (Soloski 2020). It also changes some of the main characters in order to get more viewership. For example, Bernard is too pompous in the novel and has been 'softened' in the series, and 'John is prissy and deeply neurotic, anti-sex and anti-fun'. If John were left as is, says the showrunner, 'It'd be a little like taking Mike Pence to New London'. 'No one would watch that', so Weiner muscled and loosened him up (Soloski 2020). In short, the television series does what it can to sell happiness in a novel which saw a future in which happiness would not only be sold—but in which entertainment would itself be a drug.

Brave New World is often cited as 'remarkable for its accurate predictions about science and technology, economics and politics, and arts and leisure' including its extrapolations of 'future applications of genetics (IVF and cloning via Bokanovsky's Process), endocrinology (Malthusian belts), behaviourism (hypnopaedia), and pharmacology (soma)' (Woiak 2007: 107). But its accurate predictions about the politics and economics of happiness in our society may be its greatest prognostication, especially when considered in conjunction with our rampant consumerism, vacuous entertainments, and threats to democracy initiated by the resurgence of totalitarian ideology today. However, at least a couple of major aspects of Huxley's prediction did not come true: the first is the community aspect of happiness; the second is the relationship between happiness and truth. 'Everybody's happy now' (Huxley 2006: 75), wrote Huxley in *Brave New World*. But to achieve this, individualism and truth were sacrificed. Of the first, in our happy neoliberal society, everyone *does not* belong to everyone else. In fact, it is quite the opposite, with community and the sense of a common good lost in the competitive hyper-individualism of neoliberal governmentality. If there is solidarity though, it is not found today in the free market. Rather, it may be found in millions of people around the world clapping their hands in unison to the belief that happiness *is* the truth—or, more precisely, that their *individual* happiness is the truth.

Contra Huxley's predictions, it is hard not to regard as common knowledge both the hyper-individualism of neoliberalism and the identification of happiness with truth. It is the type of knowledge that some areas of contemporary theoretical inquiry work overtime to combat. In the next chapter, we will see how the relationship between happiness and truth came to be regarded as a dilemma in one contemporary line of theory. It is a position that is fundamentally opposed to the idea of selling happiness—if not also to the notion of happiness itself. Later in the chapter, the connection of individualism as it relates to happiness will also be challenged. But not with the aim reestablishing a connection between happiness and solidarity. Rather, solidarity will be connected with truth—and happiness will be dismissed merely as a fantasy of neoliberal capital.

Finally, from the vantage point of our brave new world of well-being, one where happiness under neoliberal capital has become a major commodity, the station of literature is reduced to just another of the myriad of products of the happiness industry. Moreover, when compared to the other products of the happiness industry such as the how-to books, therapist payments, drugs, workshops, apps, TED talks, web sites, positive psychology coaching, and corporate and school consultants noted earlier, literature becomes a relatively small player in a very large industry. Add to this its secondary role compared to other happiness media such as television, film, and music, the repute of literature as a product of the happiness industry is relatively minor—unless, of course, Oprah decides to make your book one of the 70 she touted on her show. But even here, its celebration is as an exemplar or tool of well-being and positive psychology, not as an aesthetic achievement. Or, in Huxley's terms, it has more in common with the 'feelies' of A. F. 632 than the writings of the Bard.

Notes

1 In perhaps the epitome of faint praise regarding Alain's popularizing work, René Wellek wrote 'Alain has his merits as a *vulgarisateur*, but hardly as an independent critic' (1992: 23).
2 Alain is here referring to a Stoic view that we should calmly accept our place in the scheme of things, striving to attain *apatheia*, a form of psychic detachment from mental and physical disturbances.
3 As evidence of this obscurity, consider that McMahon (2006), a five-hundred-plus-page history of happiness does not even mention Alain—let alone discuss the contributions of a philosopher who has been put on a par with Descartes in France.
4 In Britain at the time, there was an organisation called the Eugenics Society that was devoted to promoting the British eugenics movement.

However, Huxley was not a member of this society. It is unclear though whether this was by choice or because his residency abroad (he lived in Italy and France during this period and then moved permanently in 1937 to California) did not allow him to participate in the society (Woiak 2007: 118n55).

5 Mention of eugenics virtually drops out of Huxley's published and unpublished work after 1935 (Woiak 2007: 126).

2 Happiness, no thanks!

Psychoanalysis, philosophy, and the critique of happiness from Freud to Žižek

In spite of the optimism about happiness from Alain to positive psychology, the Great War set the tone for a much more pessimistic approach. Arguably, the *rejection* of happiness and its pursuit is one of the cornerstones of the modern condition and modernity. A good place to see this typically modern position on happiness is found in the writings of Sigmund Freud, particularly his *Civilization and Its Discontents*, which was published in 1929, a year after the release of Alain's *Propos sur le bonheur*. The psychoanalytic critique of happiness initiated by Freud would continue to be developed and refined mid-century by Jacques Lacan. And today, Slavoj Žižek carries on the psychoanalytic critique of happiness developed by Freud and Lacan. And though he approaches it from many different directions and contexts, the core tenets of Žižek's approach remain consistent: psychoanalysis establishes happiness as 'the betrayal of desire' (Žižek 2002: 58). For Žižek, happiness is 'not a category of truth, but a category of mere Being, and, as such, confused, indeterminate, inconsistent' (Žižek 2002: 59)—a position most definitely contra that of the happiness journalism of Alain and the positive psychology of Seligman.

'Our Freud', it turns out, is not the unqualified champion of happiness that Huxley positions him to be in *Brave New World*. Though Freud is linked in the popular imagination with the idea that sexual activity is associated with happiness, as we will see, he was far less enthusiastic about the possibility of happiness in modern civilisation. What Huxley is after in *Brave New World* is a 'revolution' in psychology that becomes the basis of a new form of economics and government based on happiness—albeit grounded in eugenics and elitist technocracy. Though it can be linked in ways to Freudian psychoanalysis—and its extensions in Lacan and Žižek—the government of happiness in Huxley's novel is very different. Huxley notes as much in his letter to George Orwell:

DOI: 10.4324/9781003178941-3

> The first hints of a philosophy of the ultimate revolution—the revolution which lies beyond economics and politics, and which aims at the total subversion of the individual's psychology and physiology—are to be found in the Marquis de Sade, who regarded himself as the continuator, the consummator, of Robespierre and Babeuf.
>
> (Huxley 1969: 604)

But to overcome individual psychology in the furtherance of power, totalitarian governmentality will not resort to physical violence, which Huxley finds 'arduous and wasteful' (Huxley 1969: 604) but will rather utilise various forms of psychic control, which are much easier and more efficient:

> I have had occasion recently to look into the history of animal magnetism and hypnotism, and have been greatly struck by the way in which, for a hundred and fifty years, the world refused to take serious cognizance of the discoveries of Mesmer, Braid, Esdaile, and the rest. Partly because of the prevailing materialism and partly because of prevailing respectability, nineteenth-century philosophers and men of science were not willing to investigate the odder facts of psychology for practical men, such as politicians, soldiers and policemen, to apply in the field of government. Thanks to the voluntary ignorance of our fathers, the advent of the ultimate revolution was delayed for five or six generations. Another lucky accident was Freud's inability to hypnotize successfully and his consequent disparagement of hypnotism. This delayed the application of hypnotism to psychiatry for at least forty years. But now psycho-analysis is being combined with hypnosis; and hypnosis has been made easy and indefinitely extensible through the use of barbiturates, which induce a hypnoid and suggestible state in even the most recalcitrant subjects.
>
> (Huxley 1969: 604–605)

Thus, Huxley was well aware that the psychoanalysis of Freud was not the one that formed the psychological horizon of *Brave New World.* But more fundamentally, as we will see in this chapter, neither was the view of psychoanalysis as 'curing' unhappiness—with or without drugs. In a late letter to Lady Huxley, the sculptor and writer who was married to his brother, Julian Huxley, Aldous describes Freudian psychology as treating patients 'as tho[ugh] they had no bodies—only mouths and anuses—and as tho[ugh] a multiple amphibian c[oul]d be cured of his troubles by psychology alone, and psychology of only one, not too realistic brand' (Huxley 1969: 888).

Until the end of his life, Huxley held on to the view that particular psychological methods were the most effective means for governments to enslave their citizens. In 1957, he wrote to his brother, the evolutionary biologist, Julian Huxley[1]:

> it is quite clear that a dictator who systematically made use of existing [psychological] methods and subsidized research in the refinement could, by the use of drugs, sleep-teaching, hypnosis, subliminal projection and the latest advertising techniques based upon motivational research, establish a high degree of control over his subjects and make them positively enjoy their slavery (provided of course that the slavery could be combined with a standard of living high enough to satisfy physical needs).
>
> (Huxley 1969: 837)

Again, a few year later, after attending a conference where he thought these topics would be discussed, Huxley bemoans that there was 'no mention of hypnosis, brain-washing, mind-changing drugs or hypnopaedia', that is, what he considered the basic issues of 'conscience' used to control subjects (Huxley 1969: 895).

This chapter introduces Žižek's argument for saying 'No Thanks!' to happiness both within the philosophical and psychological traditions as well as its importance as an act of public philosophy, particularly via arenas such as YouTube. As an important public advocate of a modern—and highly unpopular—'tragic' view of happiness, Žižek stands squarely against the popular position on happiness celebrated in Pharrell's song—and on Oprah's television show. Though there are other ways to term Žižek's view of happiness, 'tragic' is used here based on the importance of psychoanalysis via Greek tragedy in establishing his position—and because if Žižek is right about the pursuit of happiness, then it is a tragedy for both the happiness industry and all of those who regard happiness as *the* goal of life such as the millions of people who follow Oprah or sing along with Pharrell.

Moreover, this chapter compels us to ask: What is the price of pursuing happiness under late capitalism? Is it one worth taking? Or should we follow Žižek and reject happiness? For Žižek, as we shall see, the answer here is clear but is his argument convincing enough to undermine both the philosophical and psychological arguments in support of the pursuit of happiness? Finally, we will ask how this critique of happiness impacts the world of literature in the new millennium. We'll begin by reviewing some of the major philosophical arguments in support of the pursuit of happiness before turning to Žižek's argument against happiness and its sources.

Philosophy and the pursuit of happiness

The pursuit of happiness is a persistent theme in the Western philosophical tradition dating back to the Greeks. While the general consensus among the philosophers is that people want happiness, there is much disagreement as to the constitution or nature of happiness. Moreover, there is also the question of how to achieve happiness—or even if its achievement is possible in view of the many different obstacles that stand in the way of its fulfilment.

Of the obstacles to happiness, Blaise Pascal wrote in his *Pensées* that because 'men are not able to fight against death, misery, ignorance, they have taken it into their heads, in order to be happy, not to think of them at all' (Pascal 1932: 49). 'Despite these miseries', continues Pascal, 'man wishes to be happy, and only wishes to be happy, and cannot wish not to be so' (Pascal 1932: 49). However, his pessimism towards the pursuit of happiness led others like Adam Smith to criticise Pascal by placing him among 'those whining and melancholy moralists who are perpetually reproaching us with our happiness, while so many of our brethren are in misery' (Smith 2006: 134). Still, Pascal, who wore a spiked belt next to his skin so that he could jab himself every time he found himself enjoying a conversation, supposedly never assumed his readers were happy (Moriarty 2020: 7 & 7n11). How could they be if they felt that they were unable to fight against misery, ignorance, and death?

As Pascal's 'thoughts' bring to the fore, it is one thing to desire or wish for happiness, it entirely another thing to achieve it, especially when ethical considerations are taken into account. Consequently, philosophical discussions of happiness often hinge upon what we desire regarding happiness versus what is our moral duty. Immanuel Kant makes this the centrepiece of his discussion of the pursuit of happiness. For Kant, even though 'happiness is the condition of a rational being in the world' (Kant 1949b: 227), when considering questions of morality, we should not give *any* consideration to happiness. Nevertheless, when considerations of happiness result in moral problems, the moral law must be consulted to resolve them.

As an ideal of the satisfaction of all desires, happiness is a concept whose content for Kant is so fluctuating that no moral imperative can be derived from it. He writes,

> all elements which belong to the concept of happiness are empirical, i.e., they must be taken from experience, while for the idea of happiness an absolute whole, a maximum, of well-being is needed in my present and in every future condition.
>
> (Kant 1949a: 77)

'In the doctrine of happiness empirical principles constitute the entire foundation', says Kant, 'but in the doctrine of morality they do not form even the smallest part of it' (Kant 1949b: 198). He concludes, 'one must never consider morals itself as a doctrine of happiness, i.e., as an instruction in how to acquire happiness' (Kant 1949a: 233). For Kant, morals are not 'the doctrine of how to make ourselves happy but of how we are to be *worthy* of happiness' (Kant 1949a: 232).

'To secure one's own happiness is at least indirectly a duty', argues Kant, 'for discontent with one's condition under a pressure of many cares and amidst unsatisfied wants could easily become a great temptation to transgress duties' (Kant 1949a: 60). 'But', continues Kant, 'without any view to duty, all men have the strongest and deepest inclination to happiness, because in this idea all inclinations are summed up' (Kant 1949a: 60). As such, duty and happiness are at odds with each other in Kant. 'Man feels in himself a powerful counterpoise against all commands of duty which reason presents to him as so deserving of respect', writes Kant, 'this counterpoise is his needs and inclinations, the complete satisfaction of which he sums up under the name of happiness' (Kant 1949a: 64). 'Virtue and happiness constitute the possession of the highest good in one person', says Kant. Virtue, as the worthiness to be happy, is the 'supreme condition of whatever appears to us to be desirable and thus of all our pursuit of happiness and consequently', for Kant, 'is the supreme good' (Kant 1949b: 215).

In a way, the pessimism regarding happiness in Pascal and the dissociation of happiness from ethics in Kant are a good prequel to Žižek's own antagonistic position on the pursuit of happiness—even if his own work is directly founded on the much later psychoanalysis of Freud and Lacan (if not as well by Hegelian Marxist association with Adorno and Horkheimer's grim prospect for happiness within consumer culture). However, Pascal and Kant, though important to the larger (and somewhat bleaker) picture of the pursuit of happiness in the Western tradition, are not the philosophical positions that are the main target of Žižek's attacks on happiness. Rather, these positions are best exemplified in the virtue theory of Aristotle, the social and political philosophy of John Locke, and the eudaimonistic utilitarianism of John Stuart Mill.

For Aristotle, the virtues are those characteristics that enable human beings to live well in communities. Virtue is the ability to be reasonable in our actions, desires, and emotions. Anyone who manages their skills and their opportunities well is considered virtuous. For Aristotle, all human beings seek happiness and being virtuous is what makes us happy—it enables us to achieve a state of *eudaimonia*, which is translated as both well-being and happiness.

Eudaimonia refers to the objective character of one's life rather than to a particular psychological state. Aristotle believed that human beings are happy if they perform their human 'function' well and that the function of human beings is to act in accordance with reason. Furthermore, it is reason that controls human emotions and other non-rational indicators like the desire for pleasure so that we avoid both excess and deficiency and, thus, act virtuously. In addition, individual *eudaimonia* requires proper social institutions as well as good character. Consequently, ethics, for Aristotle, is taken to be a branch of politics. However, unlike Jeremy Bentham who famously equates happiness solely with 'pleasure and the absence of pain' (1843: 214), Aristotle does not believe that happiness is pleasure, nor is it honour or wealth. Rather, happiness is an activity of the soul in accordance with virtue. Right habits are acquired by living well, and these habits are, in fact, virtues. These virtues are the best guarantee to the happy life.

Aristotle distinguishes between two types of virtues: moral and intellectual. Intellectual virtues may be taught, whereas moral virtues must be lived in order to be learned. Moral virtue comes from habit, and generally is a state of character that is a mean between the vices of excess and deficiency. This concept of moderation, or the Golden Mean, is at the heart of Aristotle's virtue theory. Courage, for example, is presented as a virtue that is a mean between the extremes of rashness (an excess) and cowardice (a deficiency). While the moral virtues are important part of the achievement of a state of well-being, it is the intellectual virtues found in the activity of contemplation or reason that produce the most perfect happiness. Nevertheless, while the contemplative life is the ultimate happy life, Aristotle says that it does not hurt to have friends, money, and good looks. In fact, in the *Nicomachean Ethics*, he argues that friends are *necessary* for happiness: 'a friend, being another self, furnishes what a man cannot provide by his own effort' (Aristotle 1941: 1088). Moreover, 'it seems strange', argues Aristotle, 'when one assigns all good things to the happy man, not to assign friends, who are thought the greatest of external goods' (Aristotle 1941: 1088).

Whereas Aristotle's view of happiness emphasises the whole person, rather than individual actions, critics of it argued that people turn to ethics to answer questions about the morality of action. When faced with a concrete moral problem, they want to know what to do, not what kind of character they should cultivate over a lifetime. Unlike, say, the deontological moral theory of Kant, Aristotle's virtue ethics does not answer common moral questions such as 'What should I do now in this situation?' One might respond to this criticism of Aristotle's ethics by saying that this is the wrong question to ask. 'What would a virtuous or decent person do now in this situation?' is the right question. If one asked the question in this way, then virtue ethics would be able to provide a response *and* a complete philosophical account of happiness. So, if Kant speaks to happiness, but distances it from moral deliberation, and Aristotle's concept of *eudaimonia* cannot account for the morality of actions, then the utilitarianisms of Bentham and Mill might be viewed as moral theories that place happiness at the centre of moral deliberation on actions.

Mill explains morality in terms of the principle of utility, or the greatest happiness principle. According to the principle of utility, we should attempt to produce the greatest balance of happiness over unhappiness. However, Mill sought to differentiate his brand of utilitarianism from that of his predecessor and mentor, Bentham, the 'father' of utilitarianism. Around the age of 14, Mill discovered the philosophy of Bentham, whose works gave him 'a creed, a doctrine, a philosophy … a religion' (Mill 1957: 44).

One of the major differences between Bentham's utilitarianism and Mill's is that Bentham's is based on considerations regarding the *quantity* of pleasure or pain (intensity, duration, certainty, proximity, fecundity, purity, and extent), whereas Mill's is focused on the *quality* of pleasure or pain, distinguishing the *higher* human pleasures from the *lower* human pleasures. Whereas Bentham's utilitarianism made the criterion of ethics the production of the greatest amount of pleasure and the least amount of pain, Mill makes a distinction between 'higher pleasures' which are of more value, and 'lower pleasures' which are of lesser value. Mill, then, unlike Bentham, distinguishes between happiness and mere sensual pleasure. 'It is better to be a human being dissatisfied than a pig satisfied' said Mill, 'better to be Socrates dissatisfied than a fool satisfied' (Mill 1976: 9). Whereas Bentham tells us to maximise the sum of pleasure, Mill tells us to maximise the sum of *higher* pleasure. Consequently, Mill's utilitarianism is sometimes called *eudaimonistic* utilitarianism to distinguish it from Bentham's *hedonistic utilitarianism*, which stems from *hēdonē*, the Greek word for 'pleasure'. Žižek, as we will see, will characterise mainstream approaches to happiness as drawing on the traditions of Bentham's hedonistic utilitarianism by describing happiness as 'spiritualized hedonism' (Žižek 2009: 54).

But even though the pursuit of happiness had been a philosophical concern of moral philosophers since Aristotle, it should be noted again that interest in happiness became a widespread 'obsession' in the eighteenth century. This obsession was one that was taken up not just by philosophers in treatises, but also allegories, dramatic poems, epistles, journals, letters, periodical essays, and prose fiction (Norton 2008: 211). In short, few philosophical problems were more popular in the eighteenth century than the problem of happiness. In fact, it has been said that Samuel Johnson chose the topic of happiness for *Rasselas* (1756) because he knew it would sell well and make him money to pay off some little debts (Norton 2008: 211). The entire book was written in the evenings of one week and earned him one hundred pounds for the first edition, and 25 more for the second edition (Johnson 1889: 6). Johnson's book put to the test the Enlightenment assumption that the aim of life is uninterrupted pleasure and satisfaction (Hudson 1996: 50). Johnson's character Rasselas 'surveys the traditional options for securing happiness: the pleasure-seeking of youth, the pastoral life in the country, the enjoyment of wealth, the life of the hermit, the philosopher who extols nature, the might of the powerful, the delights of marriage and children', and finds in each of them a lack of 'felt and constant satisfaction' (Hudson 1996: 50). Similar to *Rasselas*, Voltaire's *Candide* (1759) finds approaches by philosophers to happiness lacking. However, where Johnson calmly converses with various philosophical positions on happiness, Voltaire satirises them: to wit, Pangloss never gives up the claim that he lives in the 'best of all possible worlds' even after he has lost some important parts of his body, was hanged at an auto-da-fé, and was flogged at the bench of a Turkish galley (Voltaire 1947: 10). Both Voltaire and Johnson—along with the earlier work of Pascal—foreshadow the cynicism about happiness that would come later. Each finds the pursuit of happiness to spread 'confusion' about the value of politics, commerce, religion, education, marriage, and pleasure (Hudson 1996: 49).

Still, it was in this period that 'happiness became a right, something to which we are entitled, an idea that superseded the idea of duty'

(Hazard 1963: 24). The eighteenth-century obsession with happiness refocused the questions of the 'goodness' of man to those concerning the 'happiness' of man:

> Inasmuch as it was the aim and object of all intelligent beings, the centre on which all their activities were focused; inasmuch as it was the primary object of desire; inasmuch as the statement 'I want to be happy' was the first article of a code far older than any written law, than any religious creed, people now gave up asking themselves whether they deserved happiness; they asked whether they were getting the happiness to which they were entitled.
>
> (Hazard 1963: 24)

In politics, the US Declaration of Independence from 1776 gave its citizens the 'unalienable' right to the pursuit of Happiness, and the preamble of the French Declaration of the Rights of Man and the Citizen from 1789 states that '*au bonheur de tous* [the happiness of all]' (Déclaration 1789; Declaration 1789) is the goal of society.

In France, this promise of *common* or *public* happiness in the eighteenth century fuelled the discourse of the French Revolution. These changes were captured in the famous statement 'Happiness [*le bonheur*] is a new idea in Europe' made by the Jacobin leader Louis Antoine Saint-Just in 1794.[2] However, in spite of its fame, some commentators have pointed out that Saint-Just's statement is not true: *le bonheur* was an idea that could be traced back to seventeenth-century France (Ionescu 1984: 80). What was true and new though in France at the time of Saint-Just's statement was the idea of *political* happiness.[3] Saint-Just describes the nature of public happiness as follows:

> We have promised you the happiness of Sparta and that of Athens in their heyday; we have promised happiness of virtue and mediocrity, the happiness which springs from the enjoyment of what one needs, and without excesses; we have promised you a happiness made of the hatred of tyranny, of the delights of the cottage and of a fertile field tilled by your own hands. We promised to the people the happiness of being free and undisturbed so as to enjoy in peace the fruits and the customs of the Revolution; that of going back to nature, to morality and to found the Republic.
>
> (Saint-Just 1794 cited by Ionescu 1984: 80)

Finally, the politics of common or public happiness is captured well in another famous statement—or better yet, warning—from the same year by Saint-Just: 'You will perish, you who run after wealth and who try to find happiness other than that of the people' (Saint-Just cited by Ionescu 1984: 80). In short, Saint-Just was dedicated to the notion that happiness as a 'new' (political) idea must be kept public, rather than become the private province of individuals or groups, which might be associated with the 'old' idea.

In many ways, the utilitarianisms of Bentham and Mill noted above which formulate a moral and political philosophy based on a calculus of happiness might be viewed as the fruition of the Enlightenment writings of revolutionary French thinkers including *les philosophes*. But we would be remiss if we did not also acknowledge the role of Locke in the formation of this moral and political philosophy grounded in public happiness. Not only did this seventeenth-century English philosopher influence eighteenth-century French political thought on the pursuit of happiness but also the Anglo-American political tradition.

In his *An Essay Concerning Human Understanding*, Locke creates an equivalency, 'Satisfaction, Delight, Pleasure, Happiness, *etc.* on the one side; or Uneasiness, Trouble, Pain, Torment, Anguish, Misery, *etc.* on the other', saying that 'they are still but different degrees of the same thing, and belong to the *Ideas* of *Pleasure* and *Pain*, delight or uneasiness' (Locke 1975: 128–129). For Locke, happiness then is viewed in opposition to misery: '*Happiness* and *Misery* are the names of two extremes, the utmost bounds whereof we know not' (Locke 1975: 258). As such, happiness

> is the utmost Pleasure we are capable of, and *Misery* the utmost pain: And the lowest degree of what can be called *Happiness*, is so much ease from all Pain, and so much present Pleasure, as without which any one cannot be content.
>
> (Locke 1975: 258)

Moreover, 'though all Men desire happiness', Locke also believes that 'every one does not place his happiness in the same thing, or chuse the same way to it' (Locke 1975: 258). In other words, though everyone pursues happiness, some choose to pursue what is 'Good' in fulfilment of their individual happiness, while others pursue what is 'Evil'. Locke's response to the ultimate relativism of happiness is this: 'And to this I say, that the various and contrary choices, the Men make in the World, do not argue, that they do not all pursue Good' (Locke 1975: 258).

Locke's comments on the pursuit of happiness in his *Essay* became one of the chief sources of the political ideas underlying both the English Revolution of 1688 and the American Revolution of 1776. He is often called the 'theorist' of the English Revolution and the direct source for the US Declaration of Independence. 'So close is the Declaration of Independence to Locke in form, phraseology, and content, that Jefferson was accused of copying the *Second Treatise* [*of Government*]' (Peardon 1952: xx), which Locke published in 1690 but had worked on for ten years. As one critic puts it, 'Locke's individualism, his glorification of property rights and his love of conscience have been interwoven into the economic and social texture of American life' (Larkin 1930: 171). But so too is his conception of the pursuit of happiness 'interwoven into the economic and social texture of American life'—albeit by a crooked path.

Locke argued that governments are instituted to secure our rights to life, liberty, and *property*. And, indeed, an earlier draft of the Declaration of Independence included the pursuit of 'property', but not 'happiness'. The final version, though, as most know, goes as follows: 'We hold these truths to be self-evident, that all men are created equal; that they are endowed by their Creator with certain unalienable rights; that among these are life, liberty, and the pursuit of happiness'. In the process of working out a draft that would meet the needs of both the Northern and the Southern states, Jefferson changed 'property' to 'happiness' at the insistence of the Southern states. 'Property' at the time was Southern code for 'slaves'. The original draft therefore implied to the Southern states that slaves had the same 'unalienable rights' as those who owned them. This original draft of the Declaration of Independence was therefore viewed as anti-slavery by the Southerners.

But what still goes unexplained is *why* Jefferson chose the pursuit of 'happiness' as a substitute for 'property'. The explanation though is right there in Locke's *Essay* where he argues amidst his discussion of the nature of happiness and its pursuit that 'The necessity of pursuing true happiness [is] the foundation of Liberty' (Locke 1975: 25). Here is the full passage by Locke that connects the pursuit of happiness to the foundation of Liberty:

> As therefore the highest perfection of intellectual nature, lies in a careful and constant pursuit of true and solid happiness; so the care of our selves, that we mistake not imaginary for real happiness, is the necessary foundation of our *liberty*. The stronger ties, we have, to an unalterable pursuit of happiness in general, which is our greatest good, and which as such our desires always follow, the more are we free from a necessary compliance with our desire,

> set upon any particular, and then appearing preferable good [sic], till we have duly examin'd, whether it has a tendency to, or be inconsistent with our real happiness; and therefore till we are as much inform'd upon this enquiry, as the weight of the matter, the nature of the case demands, we are by the necessity of preferring and pursuing true happiness as our greatest good, obliged to suspend the satisfaction of desire in particular cases.
>
> (Locke 1975: 266)

While the real reason as to why Jefferson changed 'the pursuit of property' to 'the pursuit of happiness' is not known, given that the Declaration of Independence was already close in language, style, and conception to Locke's work, it is not much of a stretch to believe that Jefferson knew of the importance of happiness to liberty from the *Essay*. We will come back to the pursuit of happiness in the Declaration of Independence shortly when we turn to Žižek's critique of happiness, which uses the shift by Jefferson from property to happiness as part of his case against happiness. It might be noted here that Huxley viewed the 'soma habit' in *Brave New World* as connected to Jefferson's work here. For Huxley, soma was 'not a private vice; it was a political institution, it was the very essence of the Life, Liberty and Pursuit of Happiness guaranteed by the Bill of Rights' (Huxley 2006: 69). But now, let's turn our attention to the psychoanalytic critique of happiness as posited by Freud and Lacan, which along with the happiness industry discussed in the previous chapter, is a key component of Žižek's critique of happiness.

Psychoanalysis against happiness

As we saw earlier, the happiness industry is large and growing larger by the day. Science and industry are working day and night so that happiness pursues us wherever we go. More and more data are being collected that will make the science of happiness as predictive as the laws of physics. All of this is good news for the scientists and industries devoted to the study of happiness. But what if there is no such thing as happiness? Or what if the early Greeks like the Athenian statesman and poet Solon, who was born 250 years before Aristotle, were right when they said that a man *is* happy only when he is dead? 'Until he is dead', says Solon, 'keep the "happy" in reserve'. 'Till then', continues Solon, 'he is not happy, but only lucky' (Herodotus 1972: 53).

For someone like Aristotle, who believed that happiness was an activity, Solon's position is clearly absurd.[4] But there are also those in the philosophical tradition that are critical or even fearful of happiness. As noted at the beginning of this chapter, the rejection of happiness—*not* its pursuit—is one of the cornerstones of the modern condition and modernity. The work of Freud is one of the best sources for this position on happiness, especially one of his later works, *Civilization and Its Discontents*, which also provides a segue via Lacan to Žižek's psychoanalytic critique of happiness.

Very early in his career, while working with Josef Breuer on their jointly published *Studies on Hysteria*, Freud writes of a common objection to his treatment by patients:

> Why, you tell me yourself that my illness is probably connected with my circumstances and the events of my life. You cannot alter these in any way. How do you propose to help me, then?
>
> (Freud 1966: 351)

To which Freud replies:

> No doubt fate would find it easier than I do to relieve you of your illness. But you will be able to convince yourself that much will be gained if we succeed in transforming your hysterical misery into uncommon unhappiness. With a mental life that has been restored to health you will be better armed against that unhappiness.
>
> (Freud 1966: 351)

It is important to note, given the physiological discussions of happiness noted previously that in the last line in the above passage 'mental life' appeared as 'nervous system' in German editions of Freud's work prior to 1925 (Freud 1966: 351n1). It has been said 'in 1895 Freud was at the half-way stage in the process of moving from physiological to psychological explanations of psychopathological states' (Strachey 1966: xxv). If so, he was also halfway in the process of moving from physiological to psychological explanations of happiness—and unhappiness. But it is really with the introduction of the 'destructive instinct' or the death drive that Freud places something other than happiness as the goal of life.

In *Beyond the Pleasure Principle*, which was first published in 1920, 25 years after his work with Breuer, Freud introduces the death instinct.

> If we are to take it as a truth that knows no exception that everything living dies for *internal* reasons—becomes inorganic

> once again—then we shall be compelled to say that 'the goal of all life is death,' and, looking backwards, that 'what was inanimate existed before what is living'.
>
> (Freud 1950: 50)

He would later formally link the 'love instinct' (Eros) to the 'death instinct' (Thanatos). Together, they are the only basic instincts.

> The aim of the first of these basic instincts is to establish even greater unities and to preserve them thus—in short, to bind together; the aim of the second, on the contrary, is to undo connections and so to destroy things.
>
> (Freud 1949: 20)

For Freud, 'the final aim of the destructive instinct is to reduce living things to an inorganic state' (Freud 1949: 20). Along with these two primal forces is the 'pleasure principle', which Freud describes as 'a tendency operating in the service of a function whose business it is to free the mental apparatus from excitation or to keep the amount of excitation in it constant or to keep it as low as possible' (Freud 1950: 86). As to whether the pleasure principle

> requires a reduction, or perhaps ultimately the extinction, of the tension of the instinctual needs (that is, a state of *Nirvana*) leads to problems that are still unexamined in the relations between the pleasure principle and the two primal forces, Eros and the death instinct.
>
> (Freud 1949: 109)

So, while we have the unexamined potential for Nirvana in Freud, what about happiness?

In *Civilization and Its Discontents*, Freud leaves no doubt as to his position on happiness. While it can hardly be doubted that people 'seek happiness, they want to become happy and to remain so' (Freud 1955: 27), this conflicts with both our basic instincts and the world. According to Freud,

> the pleasure-principle draws up the programme of life's purpose. This principle dominates the operation of the mental apparatus from the very beginning; there can be no doubt about its efficiency, and yet its programme is in conflict with the whole world, with the macrocosm as much as with the microcosm. It simply cannot be put into

> execution, the whole constitution of things runs counter to it; one might say the intention that man should be 'happy' is not included in the scheme of 'Creation'. What is called happiness in its narrowest sense comes from the satisfaction—most often instantaneous—of pent-up needs which have reached great intensity, and by its very nature can only be a transitory experience. When any condition desired by the pleasure-principle is protracted, it results in a feeling only of mild comfort; we are so constituted that we can only intensely enjoy contrasts, much less intensely states themselves. Our possibilities of happiness are thus limited from the start by our very constitution. It is much less difficult to be unhappy.
>
> (Freud 1955: 27–28)

For Freud, not only does the present state of civilisation 'inadequately provide us with what we require to make us happy in life' (Freud 1955: 92), so too does 'the scheme of "Creation"'. Thus, while unhappiness is readily attainable, happiness is not. To expect otherwise goes against the fundamental tenets of psychoanalysis.

In psychoanalysis, Lacan would continue to develop in novel ways the critique of happiness that Freud initiated. For Lacan, 'Freud leaves no doubt, any more than Aristotle, that what man is seeking, his goal, is happiness' (Lacan 1997: 13). However, referring to the passage above by Freud about the conflict between happiness and the world, writes Lacan, 'I prefer to read in *Civilization and Its Discontents* the idea Freud expresses there concerning happiness, namely, that absolutely nothing is prepared for it, either in macrocosm or microcosm' (Lacan 1997: 13). For Lacan, this is the 'completely new' point Freud makes about a very old topic.

Lacan makes a major point about the limits of happiness by turning to the story of Oedipus, a man who is preordained to kill his father (King Laius of Thebes) and marry his mother (Queen Jocasta of Thebes). In the final lines of the play, the chorus provides an ominous warning regarding happiness:

> *Chorus*
>
> Citizens of Thebes, this was Oedipus,
> A man strong in war, gentle in peace.
> God gave him joy, God gave his loins increase.
> His happy lot was fire to the envious,
> But not the flutes are stilled, the trumpets cease.
> Misfortune's waves have crashed, tumultuous,

> Over that head endowed with masteries.
> He yields to the Destroyer's animus.
> A last day is reserved to all of us.
> Look to it always. Human happiness
> Is not for human error to assess.
> Call no man happy till his days surcease,
> Till all the gods of pain declare release,
> Fate turns her back upon his obsequies,
> And happiness may rest with him in peace.
>
> (Sophocles 1972: 80)

Freud, of course, uses this story to establish the Oedipus complex, a cornerstone of his psychoanalysis. In boys, Freud describes the Oedipus complex as one

> in which he desires his mother and would like to get rid of his father as being a rival, develops naturally from the phase of his phallic sexuality. The threat of castration compels him, however, to give up that attitude. Under the impression of the danger of losing his penis, the Oedipus complex is abandoned, repressed and, in most normal cases, entirely destroyed, and a severe super-ego is set up as its heir.
>
> (Freud 1965: 129)

For Freud, the role of castration in the Oedipus complex, as noted above, is also linked to Sophocles's tragedy. In *An Outline of Psychoanalysis*, Freud says that 'the blinding with which Oedipus punished himself after discovery of his crime is, by the evidence of dreams, a symbolic substitute for castration' (Freud 1949: 92fn11).

It is also worth noting that the Oedipus complex is not just reserved for boys. It also occurs in girls; however, it 'is almost the opposite' in girls as it is in boys. Writes Freud,

> The castration complex prepares for the Oedipus complex instead of destroying it; the girl is driven out of her attachment to her mother through the influence of her envy for the penis and she enters the Oedipus situation as though into a haven of refuge. In the absence of fear of castration the chief motive is lacking which leads boys to surmount the Oedipus complex. Girls remain in it for an indeterminate length of time; they demolish it late and, even so, incompletely. In these circumstances the formation of the super-ego must suffer; it cannot attain the strength and independence which

> give it its cultural significance, and feminists are not pleased when we point out to them the effects of this factor upon the average feminine character.
>
> (Freud 1965: 129)

For Freud, these Oedipus complexes mark the first time that 'the differences between the sexes find psychological expression' (Freud 1949: 88–89).

But unlike Freud, who uses the story to establish the Oedipus complex, a cornerstone of his psychoanalysis, Lacan says that 'in a sense Oedipus did not suffer from the Oedipus complex' (Lacan 1997: 304). 'He simply killed a man', continues Lacan, 'whom he didn't know was his father' (Lacan 1997: 304). However, rather than abandoning the myth in his psychoanalysis, Lacan reinterprets it to show the conflict between happiness and knowledge:

> [Oedipus] doesn't know that in achieving happiness, both conjugal happiness and that of his job as king, of being the guide to the happiness of the state, he is sleeping with his mother. One might therefore ask what the treatment he inflicts on himself means. Which treatment? He gives up the very thing that captivated him. In fact, he has been duped, tricked by reason of the fact that he achieved happiness. Beyond the sphere of the service of goods and in spite of the complete success of this service, he enters into the zone in which he pursues his desire.
>
> (Lacan 1997: 304)

For Lacan, the tragedy of Oedipus is not the desire for his mother, but rather his desire to know. Happiness then leads Oedipus to pursue the desire to know to its end, which then leaves him 'to deal with the consequence of that desire that led him to go beyond the limit, namely the desire to know' (Lacan 1997: 305). 'He has learned', comments Lacan, 'and still wants to learn something more' (Lacan 1997: 305). But, as the Chorus Leader in Sophocles's tragedy warns, 'We must not try to understand *too* much' (Sophocles 1972: 80).

Nevertheless, writes Lacan, in our own time 'happiness has become a political matter' (Lacan 1997: 292), by which he means that it is regarded as a right of the people (as in the United States and French Declarations). And because of this,

> the question of happiness is not susceptible to an Aristotelian solution, that the prerequisite [for happiness] is situated at the

> level of the needs of all men. Whereas Aristotle chooses between the different forms of the good that he offers the master, and tells him that only certain of these are worthy of his devotion—namely, contemplation—the dialectic of the master has, I insist, been discredited in our eyes for historical reasons that have to do with the period of history in which we find ourselves. Those reasons are expressed in politics by the following formula: 'There is no satisfaction for the individual outside of the satisfaction of all'.
>
> (Lacan 1997: 292)

For Lacan, this is the context of analysis circa mid-twentieth century. It is also the context 'that the analyst sets himself up to receive, a demand for happiness' (Lacan 1997: 292). 'To refocus analysis on the dialectic makes evident the fact that the goal is indefinitely postponed', writes Lacan. 'It's not the fault of analysis if the question of happiness cannot be articulated in any other way at the present time' (Lacan 1997: 292). Moreover, whereas for Aristotle, there *was* a discipline of happiness, for Lacan, at the present moment in history, we are 'far from any formulation of a discipline of happiness' (Lacan 1997: 292). For him, happiness is a 'bourgeois dream' and the analyst that guarantees 'the possibility that a subject will in some way be able to find happiness even in analysis is a form of fraud' (Lacan 1997: 303). Nevertheless, 'we do not disclaim our competence to promise happiness in a period in which the question of its extent has become so complicated' as a political factor (Lacan 1977a: 252). 'To be fair', says Lacan to his colleagues, 'the progress of humanism from Aristotle to St Francis (of Sales) did not fill the aporias of happiness either' (Lacan 1977a: 252). In short, in spite of these pragmatic remarks to his colleagues regarding happiness in psychoanalysis, Lacan finds himself at odds with the American psychology on this topic.

In his report to the Rome Congress in 1953, Lacan says that the behaviourism of American psychology is 'at the antipodes of the psychoanalytic experience' (Lacan 1977b: 37–38). He contends that behaviourism 'so dominates the notion of psychology in America that it has now completely obscured the inspiration of Freud in psychoanalysis itself' (Lacan 1977b: 38). His description of psychoanalysis in the United States to his colleagues in Rome is that it has

> inclined towards the adaptation of the individual to the social environment, towards the quest for behaviour patterns, and towards all the objectification implied in the notion of 'human relations'.

> And the indigenous [American] term 'human engineering' strongly implies a privileged position of exclusion in relation to the human object.
>
> (Lacan 1977b: 38)

A few years later, he expands on this thought in a lecture in Vienna:

> But its practice in the American sphere has been so summarily reduced to a means of obtaining 'success' and to a mode of demanding 'happiness' that it should be pointed out that this constitutes a repudiation of psychoanalysis, a repudiation that occurs among too many of its adherents from the simple, basic fact, that they have never wished to know anything about the Freudian discovery, and that they will never know anything about it, even by way of repression.
>
> (Lacan 1977c: 127–28)

For Lacan, the American way of life revolves around signifiers such as adaptation, human relations, human engineering, brain trust, success, basic personality, pattern, happy ending, and happiness. These signifiers mark the ideology of American free enterprise and are antithetical to the form of psychoanalysis he develops. 'A team of egos', writes Lacan, 'no doubt less equal than autonomous (but by what stamp of origin do they recognize each other in the sufficiency of their autonomy?), offers itself to Americans to guide them toward happiness', comments Lacan, 'without upsetting the autonomies, whether egoistic or not, that pave with their nonconflictual spheres the American way of getting there' (Lacan 1977a: 231).

Žižek against happiness

Following in the psychoanalytic footsteps of Freud and Lacan, Žižek argues that if the goal of life is happiness, then we are in for problems—*big* problems. It is an argument that he has consistently made for the past 30 years, along the way adding to it additional layers of political and cultural evidence. Though heavily steeped in Lacanian psychoanalysis, his argument is not just directed to fellow analysts and philosophers, but rather to anyone who will listen to him. And he draws our attention to his position on happiness by swimming against the strong American current in celebration and pursuit of happiness.

A recent example is the sold-out debate he had with the psychologist Jordan Peterson on the topic of happiness. Called the 'duel of the century', Žižek defends a Marxist position on happiness, whereas Peterson takes the capitalist side. But Žižek finds it ironic that the participants in this duel 'are both marginalized by the official academic community' (Žižek and Peterson 2019). He says that though he is 'supposed to defend here the left, liberal line against the neo-conservatives', he is most often attacked by left liberals. The politics of his position on happiness get even more complicated when one takes into account that he follows Lacan (who, in turn, followed Saint-Just, who was discussed earlier) in regarding happiness as a 'political factor'.

In an early work, *For They Know Not What They Do: Enjoyment as a Political Factor* (1991), he says, 'What Saint-Just meant by "happiness" has of course little to do with enjoyment: it implies revolutionary Virtue, a radical renunciation of the decadent pleasures of the *ancient régime*' (Žižek 2008a: 253–254). Ten years later, he writes in *On Belief* that 'liberalism tries to avoid (or, rather, cover up)' a paradox at the centre of this line of thought, namely, the idea that

> 'totalitarianism' imposes on the subject his or her own good, even if it is against his will—recall King Charles' (in)famous statement: 'If any shall be so foolishly unnatural as to oppose their king, their country and their own good, we will make them happy, by God's blessing—even against their wills'.
>
> (Žižek 2001: 119)

Liberals avoid the paradox of happiness as a political factor by 'clinging to the end to the fiction of the subject's immediate free self-perception ("I don't claim to know better than you what you want—just look deep into yourself and decide freely what you want!")' (Žižek 2001: 119). In short, like Lacan, Žižek's announcement of happiness as a political factor signals both a split from the Aristotelian approach to happiness and is also expressed in politics by the same formula noted above: 'There is no satisfaction for the individual outside of the satisfaction of all'.

Most appropriately, Žižek chooses the example of China in his debate with Peterson to illustrate the coming together of the three notions from the title of the debate: Happiness, Communism, and Capitalism. It also allows him to show how the Left in the twentieth century defined itself through opposition to two 'fundamental tendencies of modernity: the reign of capital with its aggressive market competition, [and] the authoritarian bureaucratic state power'. For Žižek, China combines these two features of modernity 'on behalf of the majority of the people' in an extreme form: a 'strong totalitarian state' and 'state-wide capitalist dynamics'. He then asks: 'Are the Chinese any happier for all that?' The answer here is of course 'No', which Žižek says is determined by psychoanalysis, not philosophy or economics.

Psychoanalysis shows us that 'humans are very creative in sabotaging our pursuit of happiness', says Žižek. He continues by telling the audience,

> Happiness is a confused notion, basically it relies on the subject's inability or unreadiness to fully confront the consequences of his/her/their desire. In our daily lives, we pretend to desire things, which we do not really desire, so that ultimately the worst thing that can happen is to get what we officially desire.
>
> (Žižek et al. 2019)

Elsewhere, in a YouTube video that has been viewed 1.6 million times, he repeats this line of thought and illustrates it through what he calls the 'traditional male chauvinist scenario': a married man is in a cold relationship so takes on a mistress. He dreams all the time that if my wife were to disappear it would open up new life for me with the mistress. But, says Žižek, 'every psychoanalyst will tell you what quite often happens' is that when the wife goes away, you also lose the mistress. You thought this is all you wanted, but it turns out that what you really wanted is not to live with the mistress, but 'to keep her at a distance as an object of desire about which you dream' (Žižek 2012). This, for Žižek, is how things function: 'we don't really want what we think we desire'. Ultimately, for him, happiness is an 'unethical category' (Žižek 2012).

While Žižek rails against happiness from many different directions and contexts, the core tenets of his approach remain consistent: psychoanalysis establishes happiness as 'the betrayal of desire' (Žižek 2002: 58). As psychoanalysis, at least for Žižek, 'is a kind of anti-ethics' (Žižek 2008b: 16), happiness is regarded by him as an 'unethical category' both in the sense that he doubts its veracity as a mere category *and* that he does not see it as constitutive of morality like, for example, Aristotle, Bentham, and Mill. For Žižek, happiness is 'not a category of truth, but a category of mere Being, and, as such, confused, indeterminate, inconsistent' (Žižek 2002: 59).[5] It is also a term used everywhere. Thus, it is hard for Žižek not to hit something or someone every time he swings his argument against happiness.

His targets include not just the philosophical tradition regarding the pursuit of happiness (e.g. Aristotle, Locke, Mill) but also revered religious figures like the Dalai Lama, who he says 'has had much success recently preaching the gospel of happiness around the world, and no wonder he is finding the greatest response precisely in the USA, the ultimate empire of the (pursuit of) happiness' (Žižek 2002: 59). Other major targets include fundamental Christian beliefs such as the idea of living 'happily ever after', which he says is 'a Christianized version of paganism' (Žižek 2002: 59). Happiness is 'a *pagan* concept', writes Žižek, noting that pagans believe happiness is the goal of life and 'religious experience and political activity are considered the highest forms of happiness (see Aristotle)' (Žižek 2002: 59). 'In short', concludes Žižek, '"happiness" belongs to the pleasure principle, and what undermines it is the insistence of a Beyond of the pleasure principle' (Žižek 2002: 59). The politics though of his position on happiness defy easy Left/Right classification.

For example, of conservatives, he says they are 'fully justified in legitimating their opposition to radical knowledge in terms of happiness: knowledge ultimately makes us unhappy' (Žižek 2002: 61). For Žižek, there 'is deep within each of us a *Wissenstrieb*, a drive to know' (Žižek 2002: 61). However, he also notes, 'Lacan claims that the spontaneous attitude of a human being is that of "I don't want to know about it"' (Žižek 2002: 61). As one Lacan commentator bluntly summarises this position, 'happiness amounts to the stupidity of "not wanting to know" the truth about symbolic castration, the inconsistency of the Other, and the actual lack of the Other' (Chiesa 2006: 360n17 & 361n18). As a consequence of our 'stupidity', happiness not only becomes, as noted earlier, a political factor and can mean only that 'everybody is identical with everyone else', but also that 'it is only the phallus which is happy and not its bearer' (Chiesa 2006: 360n17 & 361n18). Thus, by *fully justifying* the conservative argument for stupidity and grounding it in their pursuit of happiness, Žižek appears as siding against liberals who *fully reject* this argument because they believe that knowledge leads to happiness.

If conservatives find an ally in Žižek's assault on happiness, then liberals find an enemy. For example, one of the casualties of Žižek's assault on happiness is Jürgen Habermas. Žižek identifies Habermas as 'the great representative of the Enlightenment tradition' (Žižek 2002: 63). However, Žižek finds hidden in Habermas's argument advocating biogenetic manipulation the underlying premise 'that the ultimate ethical duty is that of protecting the Other from pain', which would include in some cases keeping the Other 'in protective ignorance' (Žižek 2002: 63). Žižek says that keeping knowledge away from the Other is not about autonomy and freedom as Habermas would have us believe, but it is really about happiness, which thus places this 'great representative of the Enlightenment tradition' on 'the same side as a conservative advocates of blessed ignorance' (Žižek 2002: 64). In short, both conservatives *and* liberals become targets through Žižek's critique of happiness because 'the opposition between Rightist populism and liberal tolerance is a false one' (Žižek 2002: 82). For Žižek, they are 'two sides of the same coin' (Žižek 2002: 82). What then should we be striving for if not happiness conservative- or liberal-style? Žižek's answer here is clear: 'not the Fascist with a human face, but the freedom fighter with an inhuman face' (Žižek 2002: 82).

To go along with this 'inhuman face', he also calls for an '"inhuman" ethics, an ethics addressing an inhuman subject' (Žižek 2008b: 16). This direction for ethics is part of his critique of the humanist ethics of the Western philosophical tradition predicated on its use of 'Man' and 'human person', which for Žižek 'is a mask that conceals the pure subjectivity of the Neighbor' (Žižek 2008b: 16), an account of subjectivity irreducible to the gentrified social ego. For him, until the mask of 'Man' and 'human person' are taken off of the Neighbor, its pure subjectivity is obfuscated in ethics. When the mask of these concepts *is* removed through the ethics of psychoanalysis, the Neighbor is revealed to have all of the connotations commonly found in horror fiction: behind every homely face lurks an evil monster waiting to come out. Žižek uses the example of Stephen King's horror novel, *The Shining* (1977), where 'a gentle failed writer … gradually turns into a killing beast [who] with an evil grin, goes on to slaughter his entire family' (2008b: 16). This is the 'pure subjectivity' that humanist ethics masks with terms like 'Man' and 'human person'.

To make this argument, Žižek reminds us that in the Judeo-Christian tradition, the 'Neighbor' is so traumatic and monstrous that Lacan applied Thing (*das Ding*) to the term—a term he borrowed from Freud who used it to designate 'the ultimate object of our desires in its unbearable intensity and impenetrability' (Žižek 2008b: 16). Both Freud and Lacan find the Judeo-Christian injunction to 'love thy neighbor' problematic because it domesticates the *inhuman* dimension of the Neighbor, that is, its pure subjectivity as 'Thing'. Though humanist ethics masks this problem with terms like 'Man' and 'human' (which transforms the Neighbor into an image of the self), Žižek argues for the rejection of all ethics that universalise disavowing the inhuman subjectivity of the Neighbor including the Judeo-Christian tradition. So, Žižek's anti-ethics (so termed to disassociate itself from both the Western philosophical and Judeo-Christian traditions), which serves as a base for his rejection of happiness, is also a rejection of humanism *and* the majority of Western ethics dating back to the Greeks.

So if taking on humanism, ethics, and the conservative and the liberal political establishment were not enough, Žižek's critique of happiness also takes on the institution of psychology. Here, he is directly following in the footsteps of his mentor, Lacan, in rejecting behavioural psychology and its contemporary instantiations, such as 'positive' psychology and the new discipline of 'happiness studies' noted in the previous chapter. For Žižek, we live in 'era of spiritualized hedonism' (Žižek 2009: 54), where happiness is regarded 'as the supreme duty' (Žižek 2008b: 22). 'No wonder', he says,

> over the last decade the study of happiness emerged as a scientific discipline of its own: there are now 'professors of happiness' at universities, 'quality of life' institutes attached to them, and numerous research papers; there is even the *Journal of Happiness Studies*.
>
> (Žižek 2008b: 44)

Since he said this in 2008, the study of happiness has not only grown exponentially but has increasingly expanded into, as Tamsin Shaw calls it, 'The New Military-Industrial Complex of Big Data Psy-Ops' (Shaw 2018). The latter includes the defence industry, British and American intelligence agencies, and companies like Cambridge Analytica, a company which Žižek says 'makes it clear how cold manipulation and the care for love and human welfare are two sides of the same coin' (Žižek 2020: 244). Žižek then beckons us to expand the critique of the happiness industry:

> The predominant critique proceeds in the way of demystification: beneath the innocent-sounding research into happiness and welfare, it discerns a dark, hidden, gigantic complex of social control and manipulation exerted by the combined forces of private corporations and state agencies. But what is urgently needed is also the opposite move: instead of just asking what dark content is hidden beneath the form of scientific research into happiness, we should focus on the form itself. Is the topic of scientific research into human welfare and happiness (at least the way it is practiced today) really so innocent, or is it already itself permeated by the stance of control and manipulation?
>
> (Žižek 2020: 246–247)

From Lacan's complaints about the rise of behavioural psychology in America to Žižek's identification of the happiness research at the core of the military industrial complex today, there is good reason to be suspicious about the pursuit of happiness. But Žižek makes an even more important point about the rise of the happiness industry, one that should not get lost in the shuffle of his theoretical arguments against happiness: though we live in an era wherein 'the goal of life is directly defined as happiness', we still see an explosion in 'the number of people suffering from anxiety and depression' (Žižek 2009: 54–55). 'It is the enigma of this self-sabotaging of happiness and pleasure' comments Žižek of this rise in cases of anxiety and depression in an age devoted to happiness that 'makes Freud's message more *pertinent* than ever' (Žižek 2009: 55, my emphasis). He repeats this last line in his 2020 essay, 'Happiness? No, thanks!' changing the word *pertinent* to *actual* (Žižek 2020: 247). All modesty aside and with due respect to Freud, it is Žižek's message about happiness that needs to be touted as not only actual and pertinent, but vital in dark times.

Conclusion

Žižek's arguments against happiness are among his most important contributions to our understanding of modernity today. If Freud's work on modern unhappiness announced one of the more important theoretical dimensions of modernity, then Žižek via Lacan can be seen as an extension and development of the project of modernity. Žižek's call to reject happiness and humanism though is not mere philosophical pessimism or antagonism in the face of a world gone 'happy', but rather a diagnosis for a world that is sick but chooses 'happiness' over knowledge nevertheless.

Still, we have only scratched the surface of the damage that the pursuit of happiness continues to inflict upon our world. Žižek explains, for example, how the kingdom of Bhutan 'decided to focus on Gross National Happiness (GNH) rather than Gross National Product (GNP)' (Žižek 2020: 247) further extending, for example, the legacies of the work of Bentham, Fechner, and Jevons to connect happiness to economics in the socio-political sphere. In the United States, Žižek's critique of happiness goes to the very core of our declaration of independence and founding principles that link the pursuit of happiness to the pursuit of humans as property, that is to say, slavery.

According to Žižek, the Declaration of Independence is where the 'US defines itself as the land of the "pursuit of happiness"' (Žižek 2020: 253) and is a 'key element of the "American (ideological) dream"' (Žižek 2008b: 466n43). He also reminds us that the phrase 'pursuit of happiness' (as discussed earlier) was negotiated into the Declaration '*as a way to negate the black slaves' right to property*' (Žižek 2008b: 466n43, his emphasis). What 'the pursuit of happiness' in the US Declaration of Independence 'stands for is not a direct promise of happiness—as a US citizen, I am guaranteed the freedom to pursue happiness, not happiness itself, and it depends on me whether I will achieve it or not' (Žižek 2020: 253). However, 'since authentic desire is never a desire for happiness', this 'amounts to something like "a desire for no-desire, a desire to compromise one's desire"', which for Žižek is nothing less than an 'abomination' (Žižek 2020: 253).

As Black Lives Matter (BLM) forges a new American revolution today, Žižek's thoughts on the contribution of the pursuit of happiness to racial injustice take on added importance. For Žižek, BLM is not about identity politics, the ways in which racial injustice denies or delimits blacks their interests and right to pursue happiness. Rather, BLM is about 'solidarity with the excluded of global capitalism', that is, the 'Neighbor' who has no place within culture (Zalloua 2020: 152). It is also about the formation of an anti-ethics wherein blacks become freedom fighters with an inhuman face; they are the embodiment of society's excluded. The 'desire for no-desire' that the US Declaration of Independence promised as our 'right' is replaced here by a fidelity to 'the Event' of BLM (Zalloua 2020: 152). Žižek describes 'the Event' as 'something shocking, out of joint that appears to happen all of a sudden and interrupts the usual flow of things; something that emerges seemingly out of nowhere, without discernible causes, an appearance without solid being as its foundation' (Žižek 2014: 2). This Event is *open to all:* blacks are not the exclusive recipients of its message. Nevertheless, while BLM as an Event is revolutionary, its power to change the course of racial and economic justice is far from guaranteed.

Ultimately though, Žižek's critique of happiness is a work of theory. And like Jacques Derrida's critique of logocentrism, which turned the metaphysics of Western philosophy on its head, so too does Žižek's critique of happiness have the potential to turn Western philosophy's ethical and socio-political traditions regarding the pursuit of happiness on their heads. While we see in figures like Kant a resistance to the pursuit of happiness in preference to the pursuit of duty, these thoughts tend to be marginalised in the broader context of where happiness is regarded 'as the supreme duty'. As Žižek says, in Kant 'ethical duty functions like a foreign traumatic intruder that from the outside disturbs the subject's homeostatic balance, its unbearable pressure forcing the subject to act "beyond the pleasure principle", ignoring the pursuit of pleasures' (Žižek 2008b: 45). Žižek contends that the same description of how ethical duty functions also holds for *desire* in

Lacan, 'which is why enjoyment is not something that comes naturally to the subject, as a realization of her inner potential, but is the content of a traumatic superego injunction' (Žižek 2008b: 45).

Given the rise of Fascism with a human face in America, Žižek's freedom fighter with an inhuman face and ethics looks to be an increasingly better alternative. So too does giving up the pursuit of happiness if it only amounts to a 'desire for no-desire'. But what of all those people around the world who danced on the Internet to the sounds of Pharrell's hit song 'Happy'? For Žižek, like Lacan, happiness is also a 'bourgeois dream'. And the Internet, for Žižek, is 'a site for the playing out of defensive fantasies that protect us from the banal normality that is our truth' (Žižek 2008b: 13). Thus, when viewed from his perspective, people dancing in celebration to the words 'happiness is the truth' are doing quite the opposite: they are celebrating their ignorance of the truth of desire. Or, more precisely, their desire for no-desire.

In this context, it seems only fitting then that the musician, producer and entrepreneur, Pharrell Williams, started 'a cultural movement dedicated to Thinkers, Innovators and Outcasts' called 'i am OTHER'—the very concept that Žižek's philosophy denies. While Pharrell uses the term OTHER to signify a difference in identity from people who are *not* thinkers, innovators, and outcasts, this use of the term is *very* different from the psychoanalytic use that Žižek deploys. Moreover, just as viewing Pharrell's different approach from Žižek to the concept of happiness mediates another layer to our account, so too do their radically different senses of 'other'.

For Lacan, the Other (with a big 'O') names the social order, the symbolic realm where meaning happens. The big Other is deeply implicated in the production of my desire. As Žižek puts it,

> the problem with human desire is that … it is always 'desire of the Other' in all the senses of the term: desire for the Other, desire to be desired by the Other, and especially desire for what the Other desires.
>
> (Žižek 2008c: 87)

The big Other is the unattainable source of desire for wholeness, which is a kind of transcendental signifier for the manifestation of desire. The Lacanian Other is behind the limitations of representation and within the realm of the inarticulable Real. However, as there is no 'Other of the Other', for Lacan and Žižek, there is no final guarantee of the symbolic order, or, as he puts it, 'There is no "big Other" guaranteeing the consistency of the symbolic space within which we dwell:

there are just contingent, punctual and fragile points of stability' (Žižek 2005: 332). This 'lack' in the Other allows the symbolic order to function and offers a way of thinking an outside or beyond the symbolic order. Ideology works by covering over this 'lack' in the Other. It phantasmatically projects the possibility of wholeness and explains the alienation of its privileged social subjects (why they aren't happy) by scapegoating, blaming marginalised others (Jews, undocumented migrants, Blacks, refugees, etc.) for their 'theft of enjoyment'. The big Other disavows the constitutive dimension of alienation and obfuscates the subject's immanent vulnerability to interruptions of the Real (what is irreducible to a symbolic representation of reality). Thus, for Pharrell to identify himself as 'the Other' takes on a whole new level of significance in view of Lacan and Žižek's position on it.

You can subscribe to 'i am OTHER' entertainment on YouTube, 'like' it on Facebook, 'follow' it on Twitter, and 'listen' to it on Soundcloud. Pharrell's multimedia creative collective was launched on May 12, 2012 as part of YouTube's one hundred million dollar original channel initiative. Nevertheless, in spite of Pharrell's efforts here in the name of 'the Other', it does not change the lack of final guarantee of the symbolic order. In short, no matter what Pharrell claims, the status of the 'big Other' guaranteeing the consistency of the symbolic space within which we dwell does not change. Happiness *is not* the truth—no matter how many times Pharrell sings it or how well it sells.

But then again, the same conditions hold for the equivalency of happiness with truth in literature. No matter how many times popular literature grounded in positive psychology reinforces the fantasy that happiness is the truth, progressive theory today moves in the opposite direction and has a very different message. The literature hawked by Oprah and cherished by the corporate publishing arm of the happiness industry as one of its commodities may contribute to the bottom line of neoliberal capital, but its bourgeois dream of happiness is decisively rejected by theory.

From the perspective of theory, literature that promotes the bourgeois dream of happiness is complicit in the furtherance of neoliberal capital. Therefore, as moving beyond neoliberal capital is one of the aims of progressive theory, literature associated with the pursuit of happiness as the aim of life must be regarded as counter to this objective. From the perspective then of progressive theory, the import of literature that promotes the pursuit of happiness must be regarded as a mere fantasy of neoliberal capital. This position of course is not going to be popular with the many consumers of the products of the happiness industry, but popularity has never been one of the goals of progressive theory. Nevertheless, as the next chapter will show, there may be a way to preserve the significance of literature in the age of neoliberal capital that rejects bourgeois fantasies of happiness by theoretically reestablishing a repressed tradition.

Notes

1 It should be noted that Julian Huxley, like his brother, was also a proponent of eugenics, although unlike Aldous who stopped writing on the topic in the 1930s, Julian would work in eugenics throughout his life. He was a Life Fellow of the Eugenics Society from 1925, its Vice-President from 1937 to 1944, and its President from 1959 to 1962.
2 'Le bonheur est une idée neuve en Europe' (Saint-Just 1984: 715).
3 For the Jacobins, 'political happiness' is called 'public happiness [*bonheur public*]' following the language of Jean-Jacques Rousseau, especially in *Du Bonheur Public* (1762) but also in *Contract Social* (2nd ed. 1762: Book IV, Ch. 8), where it was expressed as 'félicité publique' but translated as 'public happiness' (Hudson 1984: 62). Saint-Just used the latter expression with great frequency (Hudson 1984: 79 & 79n15).
4 Writes Aristotle,

> Must no one at all, then, be called happy while he lives; must we, as Solon says, see the end? Even if we are to lay down this doctrine, it is also the case that a man *is* happy when he is *dead?* Or is not this quite absurd, especially for us who say happiness is an activity.
> (Aristotle 1941: 946)

5 Žižek says here that he is putting this in Alain Badiou's terms.

3 The happiness of the text

Morality, writing, and the pursuit of pleasure from Gide to Barthes

Literary theory finds in Freud, Lacan, and Žižek a host of ways to critique happiness. Just on the basis of their work, it is possible to take down the entire happiness industry and its products. What is offered in their place is a world where happiness must always be viewed at odds with knowledge and truth. But there is also another philosophical tradition associated with happiness that connects the goal of life with pleasure, enjoyment, and delight. It is called *hedonism*. In fact, as we saw, Žižek believes that a spiritualised version of it defines the era in which we live, an era where happiness is regarded 'as the supreme duty' (Žižek 2008b: 22). Given the alleged dominance of hedonism in relation to happiness today, this chapter will examine the most well-known advocate of hedonism in twentieth-century literary theory, Roland Barthes. Our aim is ultimately to ask what Barthes's position here contributes to the status of literature today with respect to happiness—one that to this point might be described as Janus-faced in that it is at once cherished by the corporate publishing arm of the happiness industry as a commodity that contributes to the bottom line of neoliberal capital, but also abhorred by theory for its contributions to the bourgeois dream of happiness. In this chapter, it will be argued that Barthes's hedonism offers theorists in the new millennium a way to resolve this Janus-faced conception of literature with respect to happiness.

Phases and parentheses

Barthes became an unapologetic proponent of hedonism later in his career. 'Being a hedonist (since he regards himself as one)', confesses Barthes, 'he seeks a state which is, really, comfort' (Barthes 1977: 43). His adoption of hedonism was done with a full awareness that he stood alone among the literary theorists and philosophers of his time (and

DOI: 10.4324/9781003178941-4

now ours) in his explicit engagement with the hedonic tradition. In a parenthetical comment, Barthes asks '[W]ho today would call himself a hedonist with a straight face?' (Barthes 1975: 64). '[I]t can embarrass the text's return to morality, to truth: it is an oblique, a drag anchor, so to speak, without which the theory of the text would revert to a centered system, a philosophy of meaning' (Barthes 1975: 64–65). Barthes is familiar with the long history of hedonism in philosophy and calls upon it with the aim of becoming its newest chapter. Hedonism is 'a very old tradition', comments Barthes, which 'has been repressed by nearly every philosophy; we find it defended only by marginal figures, Sade, Fourier; for Nietzsche, hedonism is a pessimism' (Barthes 1975: 57).

For critics and readers of Barthes, the adoption of hedonism established a new development in his thought. Indeed, Barthes himself notes in his 1975 autobiography, *Roland Barthes by Roland Barthes* (henceforth, *Barthes by Barthes*), that the fifth and final phase to date of his life is marked by 'genre' as an interest in 'morality' (Barthes 1977: 145). He is quick to note though '*morality* should be understood as the precise opposite of ethics (it is the thinking of the body in a state of language)' (Barthes 1977: 145). By his own admission, his major 'Works' that take up this interest in morality are *The Pleasure of the Text*, which first appeared in 1973, and *Barthes by Barthes*. Together, they offer an account of Barthes's hedonic moral philosophy, that is, his theoretical reflections on morality.

However, unlike the previous three Phases of his development, namely, 'textuality', 'semiology', and 'social mythology', where one or more 'Intertext[s]' are directly attributed (Philippe Sollers, Julia Kristeva, Jacques Derrida, and Lacan for 'textuality'; Ferdinand de Saussure for 'semiology'; and Jean-Paul Sartre, Karl Marx, and Bertolt Brecht for 'social mythology'), for this fifth phase, while Friedrich Nietzsche is attributed as the sole intertext, his name is placed in parentheses. In this regard, the parenthetical citation of Nietzsche as the sole intertext of Barthes's fifth phase bookends the parenthetical citation of André Gide as the sole intertext of his first phase. Moreover, not only is the intertext of the first phase parenthetical, so too is its genre, '(desire to write)', which is the only parenthetically attributed genre. Finally, it must also be noted that unlike the 'Works' attributed to the other four phases, which are all specific books (aside from the general 'Writings on theater', which is one of three attributions for 'social mythology'), phase one makes no attribution to any particular work.

To be sure, there is consensus that Barthes's works proceeded through the four major phases or periods he lists after the first one:

social mythology, semiology, textuality, and morality. While there may be some debate as to whether these are the precise or proper terms to designate these periods in his writing, there is little debate about their periodisation. In fact, Barthes helps those who worry about how to integrate the article or book that may not seem to fit this periodisation, saying 'between periods, obviously, there are overlappings, returns, affinities, leftovers; it is usually the (magazine) articles which are responsible for this conjunctive role' (Barthes 1977: 145). Moreover, lest one make too much of the influence of the 'Intertext' of a particular period, Barthes tamps down expectations here: 'The intertext is not necessarily a field of influence; rather it is a music of figures, metaphors, thought-words; it is the signifier as *siren*' (Barthes 1977: 145).

Still, none of the above explains why Gide and Nietzsche are attributed as intertexts *parenthetically* to their respective periods, while the others are not. Barthes comments 'each phase is reactive: the author reacts either to the discourse which surrounds him, or to his own discourse, if one and the other begin to have too much consistency, too much stability' (Barthes 1977: 145). So if Sollers, Kristeva, Derrida, and Lacan are the 'sirens' for his 'textuality' phase, this means that his own works during this period are *reacting* to their works. But the sirens of Greek mythology, those half-bird and half-woman creatures, lured sailors to their *destruction* by the sweetness of their song. Is this how Barthes wants these intertexts to be regarded: as forces of destruction? And if so, might the parentheses then be regarded as statements on the relative destructiveness of the intertext within the phase?

In the case of these four persons cited as intertexts earlier, all were alive during the development of their respective period of Barthes's career. Might this be the explanation for the parenthetical Nietzsche and Gide? Well, no because Saussure, who died two years before Barthes was even born, is the sole intertext for Barthes's semiology period and is attributed non-parenthetically, whereas Gide, who died in 1951 and was alive when Barthes was publishing his early essays in *Combat* including 'Le Degré zéro de l'écriture' in 1947, is attributed parenthetically. Moreover, Barthes (again parenthetically) mentions in *Barthes by Barthes*, that he '(... actually saw him [Gide], one day in 1939, in the gloom of the Brasserie Lutétia, eating a pear and reading a book)' (Barthes 1977: 77–78). Note for later two things about this Gide comment by Barthes: first, the somewhat peculiar use of the word 'actually' and second, that Gide was eating a 'pear', the same fruit that Augustine of Hippo stole, which has come down through intellectual history to be associated with guilt and disobedience ('The evil in me was foul, but I loved it', wrote Augustine of the pear theft. 'I loved my own perdition and my own faults, not the things for which I committed wrong, but the wrong itself' [Augustine 1961: 47]).

Barthes adds later in *Barthes by Barthes*, '[t]he movement of his [Barthes's] work is tactical: a matter of displacing himself, of obstructing, as with bars, but not of conquering' (Barthes 1977: 172). The example he uses to illustrate the displacement of self and obstruction without conquest of his work is the aforementioned notion of 'intertext':

> It [intertext] has actually no positivity; it serves to combat the law of context; *acknowledgment* is made at a certain moment as a value, but not out of exaltation of objectivity, instead to oppose the expressivity of bourgeois art; the work's ambiguity has nothing to do with the New Criticism and does not interest him in himself; it is only a little machine for making war against philological law, the academic tyranny of correct meaning.
>
> (Barthes 1977: 172)

Barthes by Barthes, says Barthes, 'would therefore be defined as: *a tactics without strategy*' (Barthes 1977: 172). His parenthetical Nietzsche then might be regarded as an acknowledgement of the tactics of the work, that is, a fragmentary Nietzschean-style technique to inquiry into morality, but not of a specific action plan for morality (or what he called earlier 'ethics'). As a 'siren' for Barthes's morality phase, our parenthetical Nietzsche perhaps then signifies a warning sign about bourgeois morality that serves as the musical soundtrack or background music to Barthes's hedonic corpus.

In my estimation, these self-professed 'phases' and their attributions of intertexts, genres, and works say much more about Barthes's hedonism than has previously been attributed. Indeed, the consensus regarding his hedonism is that in *The Pleasure of the Text*, Barthes is a literary theorist who is establishing a theory of *textual* pleasure. But this is not his *parenthetical* project. Rather, just as Kant's 1785 *Foundations of the Metaphysics of Morals* was a prelude to his 1788 *Critique of Practical Reason*, and later, 1795 *Perpetual Peace: A Philosophical Sketch*, and Nietzsche's *Beyond Good and Evil* (1886), and *Genealogy of Morals* (1887) are a prelude to *Ecce Homo* (1888), so too is *The Pleasure of the Text* a prelude to *Barthes by Barthes*. In fact, an argument might be made that *S/Z* (1970) and *Sade, Fourier, Loyola* (1971) need to be added to this list of works as well as others. But more surprising perhaps is the linkage I'd like to propose between the two bracketed intertexts: Nietzsche and Gide, both thinkers who grappled with hedonism in their own work.

By connecting some intertextual dots, a more complete picture of Barthes's hedonism begins to emerge. It is one that says that hedonism is not a mere phase of Barthes's career, but the one constant that connects all phases of his career. Given that Barthes makes a point to connect his work with a long tradition, we will now broadly survey the hedonic tradition in philosophy and its major challenges, before turning to Barthes's contributions to it. In the process, we will come to better understand not only Barthes contributions to moral philosophy, but also how his work in this area might be understood as an important development in modern philosophy.

Nevertheless, even if the roots of Barthes's hedonism are philosophical, his aim is a literary one. Drawing upon the traditions of philosophical hedonism allows him to develop his own literary hedonism, which is ultimately something very different than the work of both his philosophical *and* literary predecessors. Rather than arguing that literature expresses happiness and that it is the reader's task to locate these expressions of happiness in the text, Barthes's literary hedonism maintains that literary criticism must focus instead on the various pleasures *of* the text—to the reader. This latter move allows literature to take on a much greater value in not only the pursuit of pleasure, but also in life in general.

The pleasurable life

Hedonism is the general view that the pursuit of pleasure is the sole aim of life. It takes its name from the Greek word for pleasure, *hēdonē*, which is also the Greek word for enjoyment and delight. According to the hedonist, the problem for philosophers is not what is the good life because everyone knows that it involves maximising pleasure, enjoyment, and delight. The problem is how to obtain this pleasure—and to avoid its opposite, pain. Hedonism thus builds its philosophy from natural experiences that are common to both humans and animals. Thus, for the hedonist, because the maximisation of pleasure is a shared view of experience, it is incumbent upon the philosopher to develop a view of life that is faithful to our experience of it. The question might now be asked if everyone already knows that the pursuit of pleasure is the sole aim of life, what then could philosophy possibly add to this? Well, according to the hedonist, without the intervention of a philosophy of hedonism, we would not have the greatest assurance that our pursuit of pleasure would be successful. Here, we need the intelligent, thoughtful, and well-reasoned work of philosophy to be better assured of maximising pleasure in our life.

Put this way, hedonism does not appear to be a philosophy that should fear repression. However, Barthes is correct in his observation that hedonism 'has been repressed by nearly every philosophy' and also that it has a long tradition. As a philosophy of life, it can be traced back at least as far as the Cyrenaics, and their founder, the ancient Greek philosopher, Aristippus (435–356 BCE). A student of Socrates, Aristippus, was born and lived in Cyrene, which is in Libya. After the death of Socrates, he opened one of the three major Socratic schools in his hometown from which the philosophical movement took its name, Cyrenaicism (the other two movements were Cynicism and Megarianism). The leaders of this school included: Aristippus's daughter, Arete; his grandson, Aristippus the younger; Bio; and Euhemerus ('Cyrenaics' 1910).

Generally speaking, Aristippus contended that good and evil are reducible to pleasure and pain and that the end of life is self-gratification. Aristippus interpreted Socrates's teaching that happiness (*eudaimonia*) is one of the ends of moral action to mean that pleasure is the sole end of life. While he emphasises immediate pleasures, he also tempers them with a measure of rational control. For him, the sole criterion of pleasure is intensity, and bodily pleasures are preferred to intellectual pleasures. Philosophy, for Aristippus, is the study of the best means of living pleasantly.

Arguably, the hedonism of Aristippus owes much not only to the influence of Socrates, but also to the circumstances of his life. Cyrene was a very prosperous and beautiful city when Aristippus resided there. The marble temples and buildings of its Acropolis were comparable to those of Athens, and it enjoyed relative peace and serenity. The citizens of Cyrene were said to be pleasure-loving and indulgent. Aristippus came from a wealthy family and enjoyed the pleasures that it brought him. On a trip to Athens to see the Olympic Games, he also made the acquaintance of Socrates and became one of his most devoted followers. After Socrates died, he travelled from place to place, charging a high fee for his teaching services, for which he has also come to be associated with the Sophists. Eventually though he resettled in Cyrene to open his own school.

Lest one get the wrong opinion of the character of Aristippus from these general details about his life including the fact that he is generally credited as being the first philosopher of hedonism, it might be useful to turn to Michel Foucault's comments on him in a lecture from 1983. Foucault begins by recounting a quote from Diogenes Laertius about him:

> Aristippus did not become angry when Dionysius spat in his face, and as he was censured for accepting Dionysius' spit, he said:

> 'Look at the fisherman, if they let themselves get drenched by the sea in order to catch a gudgeon, am I, who wants to catch a whale, unable to bear some spittle?'
>
> (Foucault 2010: 342–343)

Foucault then comments on this as follows:

> But whereas Plato's dignity did not allow him to put up with insults, Aristippus accepts Dionysius' insults. He accepts them in order to be more certain of guiding him better, as one catches a whale. Is some spittle too much to bear when one is catching a whale, a big fish, that is to say, a tyrant? But—this taking place in the general framework of what for Aristippus, Socrates, Plato, and, it seems to me, all of ancient philosophy was the general function of philosophy, that is to say, the possibility of speaking courageously and freely, and telling one's truth courageously and freely—when asked 'what benefit had he got from philosophy', Aristippus replied: 'That of being able to speak freely to everyone'.
>
> (Foucault 2010: 343)[1]

Living in Cyrene, which was about ten miles from the Mediterranean, and drawing upon his life experiences with the fisherman there to rationalise putting up with an insult that was surely an unpleasant experience, Aristippus here presents a picture of the hedonist philosopher that is both dignified and rational. But more important perhaps is the *parrēsia* Aristippus sees in philosophy: the ability it gives him to speak the truth freely.

Still, in spite of Aristippus's dignified approach to hedonism, it has been widely rejected for several reasons. From a Socratic perspective, the problem with Aristippus's philosophy is that he gets the relationship between a better person and pleasure backwards. For Aristippus, the more pleasure you are experiencing, the better you are; for Socrates, the better you are, the more pleasurable your life will be. Aristippus nevertheless warned that you must not become controlled by the pursuit of pleasure, but must rather control it. But herein lies the rub of hedonism: it is all too easy to become a slave to pleasure and its pursuit. Moreover, the pursuit of pleasure as the sole aim of life, says the critic of Cyrenaic hedonism, only leads to frustration, disillusionment, and *boredom*—not happiness.

This commentary on hedonism was most famously established by Arthur Schopenhauer, who argued that the irrational striving of the will and the fact that for him the satisfaction of the will is a contradiction in terms makes his pessimism totalising. For Schopenhauer, 'life swings like a pendulum backwards and forwards between pain and ennui' (Schopenhauer 1957: Vol. 1, 402). When the will 'lacks objects of desire, because it is at once deprived of them by a too easy satisfaction, a terrible void and ennui comes over it'; but when the will is in the throes of its unquenchable thirsts, 'the nature of brutes and man is subject to pain originally and through its very being' (Schopenhauer 1957: Vol. 1, 402). In short, Schopenhauer's pessimism regards the hedonistic life as one characterised by restlessness, boredom (*ennui*), and, ultimately, suffering.

But, for Schopenhauer, this *is* life. Our hedonism necessarily entails suffering. Moreover, as a proponent of this view of life, Schopenhauer attracted a large audience to this position. A recent and respected historian of philosophy, Frederick C. Beiser, writes of Schopenhauer,

> By the early 1860s he had become the most famous philosopher in Germany. His works not only had an appeal to the general educated public, but they also proved powerful competition for philosophy professors whose agenda was limited to the logic of the sciences. Schopenhauer had performed a remarkable feat that was the envy of the professors: he had made philosophy relevant again, so that it was asking basic questions of concern to everyone alike, not only professors interested in abstruse matters of logic.
>
> (Beiser 2014: 158–159)

So, for some, the association of boredom or *ennui* (which has the same meaning in French) with hedonism is reason enough either to modify it to avoid this consequence *or* to propose another philosophy of life. Nevertheless, a criticism of hedonism, for Schopenhauer, amounts to merely a complaint about a fact of life, namely, that it swings backwards and forwards between pain and ennui.

Hedonism after Aristippus

Cyrenaicism though is the first of *many* chapters in the history of philosophy that utilise *hēdonē* as their centrepiece. For example, there was the school founded by Epicurus in 306 BCE, which not only put the Cyrenaicists out of business but also flourished until the fifth century of the common era through the work of philosophers such as Hermarchus, Polystratus, Lucretius, Philodemus, Asclepiades, and even to some extent Cicero, all before the common era, and Diogenes of Oinoanda and Diogenianus in the second and third centuries of the common era. Much later, in the fifteenth and sixteenth centuries, Lorenzo Valla and Erasmus established the so-called Christian Epicureanism, which then influenced the 'Utopian Epicureanism' of Thomas More. In addition to Epicureanism and its variations, *hēdonē* is at the centre of Thomas Hobbes's materialism, the naturalism of eighteenth-century French *philosophes* such as Helvetius, Holbach, and de La Mettrie, and the utilitarianisms of Bentham and Mill, which were noted earlier. For that matter, it is fairly safe to contend that any materialist- or naturalist-based theory or system of human nature functions through some notion of *hēdonē*.

Among the aforementioned figures, Bentham and Mill are well known and much studied figures in contemporary philosophical circles. In fact, their utilitarianism—founded upon *hedonism*—is still one of the commonplaces of contemporary philosophical ethics. Bentham, the founder of utilitarianism, was the leader of a reform group based on utilitarian principles called the Philosophical Radicals. He argued that it is a fact of nature that the goal of individual lives is the pursuit of pleasure and the avoidance of pain. This 'Principle of Utility' is the foundation of his philosophy and is clearly articulated at the opening of Chapter 1 of *An Introduction to the Principles of Morals and Legislation* (1789/1823):

> Nature has placed mankind under the governance of two sovereign masters, *pain* and *pleasure*. It is for them alone to point out what we ought to do, as well as to determine what we shall do. On the one hand the standard of right and wrong, on the other chain of causes and effects, are fastened to their throne. They govern us in all we do, in all we say, in all we think: every effort we can make to throw off our subjection, will serve but to demonstrate and confirm it.
>
> (Bentham 2011: 111–112)

For Bentham, good is only another word for 'pleasure' and 'the absence of pain' (Bentham 1843: 214). In terms of social morality, what is the right thing to do is whatever produces 'the greatest happiness of the greatest number' (Bentham 1839: 138). We should strive in our lives to maximise pleasure and minimise pain for as many people as possible. Actions that produce the greatest amounts of pleasure are to be valued morally over actions that produce lesser amounts of pleasure. His 'hedonic' or utilitarian calculus asks us to consider the quantity of pleasure or pain resulting from our behaviour in a number of respects including its intensity, duration, and certainty. Bentham believes that this is the most rational way to settle all moral controversies (Bentham 1879, esp. Chapters 1 and 4). It should be noted that Bentham's moral philosophy is very similar to the hedonism of the ancient Greek philosopher, Epicurus. This is particularly evident in Bentham's principle of utility, which he reports as 'brand[ed] with the odious name of Epicurean' (Bentham 2011: 119).

Mill follows the broad lines of Bentham's utilitarianism but, as noted earlier, with some important qualifications. Not only does Mill reject Bentham's qualitative calculus of pleasure and pain, but also his egoistic view of human nature and appeal to enlightened self-interest. Still, Mill remains committed to the hedonism of Bentham and Epicurus:

> The creed which accepts as the foundation of morals, Utility, or the Greatest Happiness Principle, holds that actions are right in proportion as they tend to promote happiness, wrong as they tend to promote the reverse of happiness. By happiness is intended pleasure, and the absence of pain; by unhappiness, pain, and the privation of pleasure.
>
> (Mill 1976: 6)

Nevertheless, Mill, unlike Bentham, distinguishes between 'higher pleasures', which are of greater value, and 'lower pleasures', which are of lesser value. Furthermore, unlike Bentham, Mill also distinguishes between happiness and mere sensual pleasure—a thought that is perfectly captured, again, in the images of a dissatisfied Socrates versus a satisfied fool or pig (Mill 1976: 9). In defence of Epicurean hedonism (and against those who see it

> as a doctrine worthy only of swine, to whom the followers of Epicurus were, at a very early period, contemptuously likened; and modern holders of the doctrine are occasionally made the subject of equally polite comparisons by its German, French, and English assailants),

Mill says

> there is no known Epicurean theory of life which does not assign to the pleasures of the intellect, of the feelings and imagination, and of the moral sentiments, a much higher value as pleasures than to those of mere sensation.
>
> (Mill 1976: 7)

In short, Mill argues for the maximisation of not the mere sum of pleasure, but rather the sum of *higher* pleasure. Consequently, Mill's utilitarianism is sometimes called *eudaimonistic* utilitarianism to distinguish it from Bentham's *hedonistic* utilitarianism.

It is through the utilitarian philosophies of Bentham and Mill that hedonism makes its most direct philosophical route into contemporary discussions. Though not a marginal line of contemporary thinking, it is nevertheless a much-contested one. This is largely because of Bentham and Mill's incorporation of hedonism into their consequentialist ethics. And contemporary heirs to their legacy, such as Peter Singer, cannot seem to write anything that does not draw the ire of major segments of the philosophical community. Arguably, even Singer, who is one of the most well-known philosophers in America, is a marginal figure, primarily through his association with utilitarian ethics, or more specifically, his association with hedonism.

However, if a simple distinction is made, hedonism moves from the margins of contemporary thought to its centre. This distinction is between the hedonism of *ethics* and the hedonism of *psychology*. Psychological hedonism is the notion that humans always act and must act from a desire for pleasure, and ethical hedonism is the notion that humans always ought to act in whatever manner will bring them the most pleasure in the long run. Whereas the latter is a much-contested notion, the former is not. In fact, from the standpoint of behavioural psychology, psychological hedonism is a *given*.

Edwin Gantt has argued that most recent theories of cognitive psychology 'have been united by a common—though usually inexplicit and unexamined—commitment to one or another form of hedonistic explanation' (Gantt 2000: 83). Writes Gantt,

> many in contemporary cognitive psychology have simply equated rationality with hedonistic self-concern. That is to say, for many in cognitive psychology, human reasoning is, at its fundamental root, nothing more nor less a matter of self-interest, and the processes of decision-making are ultimately driven by matters of individual self-concern.
>
> (Gantt 2000: 83)

Consequently, for Gantt and others, explanation in the social sciences today is dominated by the doctrine of naturalistic hedonism. Today, naturalistic hedonism is used by the social sciences to explain everything from crime, drug addiction, and changes in sexual morality to warfare, regret, voting, marriage—and even altruism (Gantt 2000: 83).

James B. Rule even goes so far as to contend that the doctrine of naturalistic hedonism 'offers the best—and perhaps the only—hope for meaningful progress in social science' (Rule 1997: 79; cited by Gantt 2000: 84).

Moreover, running alongside naturalistic hedonism in contemporary social sciences is another central theme; namely, 'that human existence is fundamentally economic existence' (Gantt 2000: 83). 'We are, it is held', comments Gantt, '*homo economicus*, and as such, in all our interactions with others and the world we perpetually and inescapably seek to maximize our individual gains (or pleasures) and minimize our individual costs (or pain)' (Gantt 2000: 83). As such, one does not have to work hard to connect the foundations of economic Darwinism, or more fashionably, neoliberalism, to naturalistic hedonism. The eviscerating consequences of the neoliberal imperatives for corporate managerialism, instrumentalism, and rationalisation in social policy and higher education practice have already been well established by myself and others—and are in themselves enough to drive us away from any form of hedonism. Nevertheless, Barthes aims to convince us, otherwise, by offering a unique literary theoretical take on hedonism.

The hedonic turn

Late in his career, Barthes sought to revive the hedonic tradition. His prolegomenon on hedonism is *The Pleasure of the Text*, where he effectively and innovatively introduces it into literary criticism and theory. He does this by uniting notions about textual generation with then current work in literary theory and psycholinguistics. In broad terms, Barthes proposes and explores three distinct kinds of pleasure: the first is the pleasure and comfort that comes from Readerly textual fulfilment, which he terms 'plaisir'; the second is the rapture and ecstasy that comes from Writerly textual unsettlement and discomfort, which he terms 'jouissance'; and the third is the textual pleasure that comes from finding ecstatic moments in Readerly texts. In *The Pleasure of the Text*, he writes:

> Text of pleasure [*plaisir*]: the text that contents, fills, grants euphoria; the text comes from culture and does not break with it, is linked to a *comfortable* practice of reading. Text of bliss [*jouissance*]: the text that imposes a state of loss, the text that discomforts (perhaps to the point of a certain boredom), unsettles the reader's historical, cultural, psychological assumptions, the consistency of tastes, values, memories, brings to a crisis his relation with language.
>
> (Barthes 1975: 14)

But when compared to the passage that follows this passage, we see Barthes the *textualist* under the intertext of Sollers, Kristeva, Derrida, and Lacan transforming into Barthes the *moralist* under the intertext of hedonists spanning from Aristippus and Epictetus to Sade and Schopenhauer. Or, more significantly, Barthes transforming his attention from the concerns of literary theory and cultural criticism (which, for purposes of parallelism, might be termed, *art de textualité*) to philosophy in its broadest and most ancient sense, namely, one concerned with the art of living (*art de vivre*), the knowledge of how to enjoy life. Continues Barthes,

> Now the subject who keeps the two texts in his field and in his hands the reins of pleasure [*plaisir*] and bliss [*jouissance*] is an anachronistic subject, for he simultaneously and contradictorily participates in the profound hedonism of all culture (which permeates him quietly under cover of an *art de vivre* shared by the old books) and in the destruction of that culture: he enjoys the consistency of his selfhood (that is his pleasure [*plaisir*]) and seeks its loss (that is his bliss [*jouissance*]). He is a subject split twice over, doubly perverse.
>
> (Barthes 1975: 14)

The stage is now set for his full entry into the hedonic tradition in *Barthes by Barthes*, a philosophical treatise on hedonism in the guise of a postmodern autobiography.

If *The Pleasure of the Text* is a hedonics of the art of reading, then *Barthes by Barthes* is a hedonics of the art of *living* (*art de vivre*). Writes Barthes in the latter book,

> the art of living has no history: it does not evolve: the pleasure which vanishes vanishes for good, there is no substitute for it. Other pleasures come, which replace nothing. *No progress in pleasures*, nothing but mutations.
>
> (Barthes 1977: 50)

Consequently, the comfort that Barthes's hedonic *art de vivre* seeks is

> more complicated than the household kind whose elements are determined by our society; it is a comfort he arranges for himself (the way my grandfather B., at the end of his life, had arranged a little platform inside his window, so as to obtain a better view of the garden while he was working). This personal comfort might be called: *ease*.
>
> (Barthes 1977: 43)

The hedonic project of *Barthes by Barthes* is to provide both a 'theoretical dignity' and 'an ethical force' to ease (Barthes 1977: 44). Barthes notes that 'the exact antonym' of ease is 'embarrassment' (Barthes 1977: 45). In personal terms, his own desire for ease stemmed from the various embarrassments he endured in pursuit of a 'bourgeois *art de vivre*' (Barthes 1977: 45) as a child.

> This art subsisted, incorruptible, amid every financial crisis; not misery, as a family experience, but embarrassment; i.e., a terror of certain terms, the problems of vacations, of shoes, of schoolbooks, and even food. This *endurable* privation (as embarrassment always is) may account for a little philosophy of free compensation, of the *overdetermination* of pleasures, of *ease* ... His formative problem was doubtless money, not sex.
>
> (Barthes 1977: 45)

This passage reveals several important aspects of Barthes's hedonism: (1) *Money* is a source of pleasure; (2) *Sex* is a source of pleasure; and (3) Pleasure is *overdetermined*—that is to say, pleasure has many sources. Let's now look briefly at each of these in turn.

Money. Barthes rejects the approach to money of three of the most dominant 'moralisms' of his milieu: Marxism (which links money to the origins of class privilege and oppression), Christianity (which advocates poverty, arguing that money is the root of all evil), and Freudianism (which assimilates it with faeces; Barthes 1977: 45–46). Instead, Barthes follows the position of Fourier on money: money creates happiness. However,

> what is defended is not money saved, hoarded, blocked; it is money spent, wasted, swept away by the very moment of loss, made brilliant by the luxury of a production; thus money metaphorically becomes gold: the Gold of the Signifier.
>
> (Barthes 1977: 46)

This position on the 'the Gold of the Signifier' echoes his general view of realist literature that he offered in his reading of 'Sarrasine' in *S/Z*: the view that literature has no real content that guarantees its authenticity in the same way that the gold standard in banking guarantees or backs the value of currency. Barthes is saying here that the value of currency or money is derived by the conventions of its circulation not by a reserve of gold bars in a bank vault. In the same way that the circulation of the signifier comes to establish the credibility of the content and characters of literature, so too does the circulation of money establish its 'Gold-reserve-like' credibility (Thody 1977: 115).

One of Barthes's biographers notes that 'the more [money] he had, the more he needed' (Samoyault 2017: 391). Later in life, when 'the penury of his early years was far behind him', maintains Tiphaine Samoyault, 'he adopted his tastes and expenditure to what he had, leading a more luxurious life and proving very generous to his friends, thereby ensuring that he was preoccupied by money and worried about not having enough' (Samoyault 2017: 391).

In *Sade/Fourier/Loyola*, a book published a couple of years before *The Pleasure of the Text*, Barthes says that for Fourier,

> Money participates in the brilliance of pleasure ('The senses cannot have their full indirect scope without the invention of money'): money is desirable, as in the best days of civilized corruption, beyond which it perpetuates itself by virtue of a splendid and 'incorruptible' fantasy.
>
> (Barthes 1976: 85)

Money then takes the same position of hedonism in the philosophical tradition as something that is repressed:

> it is because all (civilized) Philosophy has condemned money that Fourier, destroyer of Philosophy and critic of Civilization, rehabilitates it: *the love of wealth* being a pejorative *topos* (at the price of a constant hypocrisy: Seneca, the man who possessed 80 million sesterces, declared that one must rid oneself of wealth), Fourier turns contempt into praise: marriage, for example, is a ridiculous ceremony, save 'when a man marries a very rich woman; then there is occasion for rejoicing'; everything, where money is concerned, seems to be conceived in view of this counter-discourse, frankly scandalous in relation to the literary constraints of the admonition: 'Search out the tangible wealth, gold, silver, precious metals, jewels, and objects of luxury despised by philosophers'.
>
> (Barthes 1976: 85–86)

As such, Fourier's claims are the 'basis for the major transgression against which *everyone*—Christians, Marxists, Freudians—for whom money continues to be an accursed matter, fetish, excrement, has spoken out: who would dare defend money?' (Barthes 1976: 86). This 'dare' echoes the implied dare Barthes would later make regarding hedonism: '[W]ho today would [dare] call himself a hedonist with a straight face?' (Barthes 1975: 64).

Sex. The Pleasure of the Text is an erotics of reading, whose deployment of *plaisir* and *jouissance* deals with a state (*plaisir*) and an action (*jouissance*), both of which, comments Richard Howard, 'in our culture [English], are held to be unspeakable, beyond words' (Howard 1975: vi). What Barthes calls *jouissance*, the Bible translates as 'knowing', the Stuarts called 'dying', and we call 'coming', that is, the orgasm (Howard 1975: vi). In light of these alternatives, Richard Miller's translation of *jouissance* as 'bliss', is, well, a bit sexually deflating. 'The pleasure of the text is like that untenable, impossible, purely *novelistic* instant so relished by Sade's libertine when he manages to be hanged and then to cut the rope at the very moment of his orgasm, his bliss', writes Barthes (1975: 7).

At the centre of Barthes's hedonism is the erotic body which experiences pleasure. Asks Barthes,

> Does the text have human form, is it a figure, an anagram of the body? Yes, but of our erotic body. The pleasure of the text is irreducible to physiological need. The pleasure of the text is that moment when my body pursues its own ideas—for my body does not have the same ideas I do.
>
> (Barthes 1975: 17)

Like the rationalist René Descartes, who through self-examination arrives with certainty at his existence as *res cogitans*, a thinking thing (Descartes 1967: I, 132–199), Barthes goes through a parallel process albeit to establish his own material existence as an 'individual' erotic body:[2]

> Whenever I attempt to 'analyze' a text which has given me pleasure, it is not my 'subjectivity' I encounter but my 'individuality', the given which makes my body separate from other bodies and appropriates its suffering or its pleasure: it is my body of bliss I encounter.
>
> (Barthes 1975: 62)

This body is less the *res extensa* of Descartes than the body which Bentham says Nature has provided to govern us through 'two sovereign masters, *pain* and *pleasure*'. 'My body exists', writes Barthes, 'for myself only in two general forms: migraine and sensuality' (Barthes 1977: 60). For him, '[m]igraine is merely the very first degree of physical pain, and sensuality is for the most part considered only as a kind of reject-version of active pleasure. In other words, my body is not a hero' (Barthes 1977: 60).

Through this process of establishing the existence of the erotic body, namely, the body subject to pain [*migraine*] and pleasure [*sensuality*], the subject appears to return, 'not as illusion, but as *fiction*' (Barthes 1975: 62). Continues Barthes,

> A certain pleasure is derived from a way of imagining oneself as *individual*, of inventing a final, rarest fiction: the fictive identity. This fiction is no longer the illusion of unity; on the contrary, it is the theater of society in which we stage our plural: our pleasure is *individual*—but not personal.
>
> (Barthes 1975: 62)

The last clause here emphasises difference between the 'individual', which for him is the erotic body which has returned as a fiction, and the 'personal', which for him is akin to the Gold described above, namely, that which guarantees the 'individual' in the same way that the gold standard in banking guarantees the value of currency.

Barthes believes that his erotics of the text reveals a radical materialism which connects his work to an older philosophical tradition. 'Have not the rare materialists of the past, each in his way, Epicurus, Diderot, Sade, Fourier, all been overt eudaemonists?' (Barthes 1975: 64). Still, each of these materialists composed a discourse very different from Barthes. 'What shall we call such discourse?', wonders Barthes?

> *[E]rotic*, no doubt, for it has to do with pleasure; or even perhaps: *aesthetic*, if we foresee subjecting this old category to a gradual torsion which will alienate it from its regressive, idealist background and bring it closer to the body, to the *drift*.
>
> (Barthes 1977: 84)

And, moreover, ultimately bring it closer to *materialism*.

In *Sade/Fourier/Loyola*, these themes are brought back into the context of *the art of living*, noted above:

> whenever the 'literary' Text (the Book) transmigrates into our life, whenever another writing (the Other's writing) succeeds in writing fragments of our own daily lives, in short, whenever *co-existence*

> occurs. The index of the pleasure of the Text, then, is when we are able to live with Fourier, with Sade. To live with an author does not necessarily mean to achieve in our life the program that the author traced in his books (this conjunction is not, however, insignificant, since it forms the argument of *Don Quixote*; true, Don Quixote is still a character in a book); it is not a matter of making operative what has been represented, not a matter of becoming sadistic or orgiastic with Sade, a phalansterian with Fourier, of praying with Loyola; it is a matter of bringing into our daily life the fragments of the unintelligible ('formulae') that emanate from a text we admire.
>
> (Barthes 1976: 7)

The problem of sex in Barthes's hedonism thus amounts to being able 'to live with Sade'—but not necessarily becoming sadistic or orgiastic. It is interested here to note that Aldous Huxley saw in Sade the 'first hints of a philosophy of the ultimate revolution—the revolution which lies beyond politics and economics, and which aims at the total subversion of the individual's psychology and physiology' (Huxley 1969: 604). For Huxley, 'the ruling minority in [Orwell's] *Nineteen Eighty-Four* is a sadism which has been carried to its logical conclusion by going beyond sex and denying it' (Huxley 1969: 604). In a way, Barthes 'sadism' makes a similar move to the one Huxley attributes to Orwell. The parallel is accomplished by replacing Orwell's 'boot', that is, the one that the ruling minority always has 'on-the-face', with Barthes's 'text', which now the reading minority always has on the text.

Barthes erotics of reading finds a full role for sex and sexuality in his writing without him ever having to explicitly make reference to his own sexual life or sexuality. Indeed, in all of the writing he published during his life, including his 'autobiography', his sexual life is not addressed. The posthumous publication of *Incidents* in 1987 is the first published book where he directly puts his sexual life to writing. Jonathan Culler notes that *Incidents* is 'Loosely influenced by André Gide's journal, which had narrated homosexual encounters in North Africa'. Culler says that it 'avoids narrative and presupposes rather than describes homosexual encounters in laconic fragments' (Culler 2002: 110).

Overdetermination of Pleasure. Money and sex are sources of pleasure in Barthes's hedonism. However, they are just the beginning of the long queue of potential sources of pleasure. In *Barthes by Barthes*, he discusses the pleasure of kissing (Barthes 1977: 141), embracing (Barthes 1977: 141), inserting ('Is there not a kind of voluptuous pleasure in inserting' [Barthes 1977: 135]), the endoxal products of mass culture (Barthes 1977: 141), writing beginnings/fragments ('he tends to multiply this pleasure: that is why he writes fragments' [Barthes 1977: 122]), the Political ('I believe I understand that the Political pleases me as a *Sadean* text and displeases me as a *Sadistic* text' [Barthes 1977: 147]), Haiku (Barthes 1977: 94), sexy sentences (Barthes 1977: 164), ideology (Barthes 1977: 104), contrary opinions of whether he is a Sorbonne professor (Barthes 1977: 61), calculation (Barthes 1977: 100), writing (Barthes 1977: 86), etymology (Barthes 1977: 85), piano playing (Barthes 1977: 70), perversion ('in this case, that of the two H.'s: homosexuality and hashish' (Barthes 1977: 63), friends (Barthes 1977: 65), fantasising (Barthes 1977: 88)—and his displeasure of translation, foreign literature, and foreign languages ('little taste for foreign literature, constant pessimism with regard to translation' [Barthes 1977: 115]) and dreaming ('Dreaming (whether nicely or nastily) is insipid' [Barthes 1977: 87]). At one point, he even explicitly confronts and lists, without explanations, many of the things he likes and dislikes:

> *I like:* salad, cinnamon, cheese, pimento, marzipan, the smell of new-cut hay (why doesn't someone with a 'nose' make such a perfume), roses, peonies, lavender, champagne, loosely held political convictions, Glenn Gould, too-cold beer, flat pillows, toast, Havana cigars, Handel, slow walks, pears, white peaches, cherries, colors, watches, all kinds of writing pens, desserts, unrefined salt, realistic novels, the piano, coffee, Pollock, Twombly, all romantic music, Sartre, Brecht, Verne, Fourier, Eisenstein, trains, Médoc wine, having change, *Bouvard and Pécuchet*, walking in sandals on the lanes of southwest France, the bend of the Adour seen from Doctor L.'s house, the Marx Brothers, the mountains at seven in the morning leaving Salamanca, etc.
>
> *I don't like:* white Pomeranians, women in slacks, geraniums, strawberries, the harpsichord, Miró, tautologies, animated cartoons, Arthur Rubinstein, villas, the afternoon, Satie, Bartók, Vivaldi, telephoning, children's choruses, Chopin's concertos, Burgundian branles and Renaissance dances, the organ, Marc-Antoine Charpentier, his trumpets and kettledrums, the politico-sexual, scenes, initiatives, fidelity, spontaneity, evenings with people I don't know, etc.
>
> (Barthes 1977: 116–17)

The field of pleasure established by Barthes in *Barthes by Barthes* is vast, diverse, and idiosyncratic. These are not things that every hedonist *should* like (or dislike), rather they represent the likes (and dislikes) of one (and only one) hedonist: Roland Barthes. 'The important thing', writes Barthes, 'is to equalize the field of pleasure, to abolish the false opposition of practical life and contemplative life' (Barthes 1975: 59). The listing here and the various pleasures (and displeasures) described throughout the book establish both the relativity (likes and dislikes are individual) and the flatness of pleasure in Barthes's hedonism: there are no higher and lower pleasures here—the pleasures of the body are on the same level as the pleasures of the mind. Still, pleasures can and should be regarded differently. For example, '[w]riting is a dry, ascetic pleasure, anything but effusive' (Barthes 1977: 86). Thus, the paradox of pleasure in Barthes: all pleasures are equal but not the same.

For many philosophers, a paradox like this at the centre of their philosophy might be regarded as a problem. But not for Barthes. His pluralistic approach to pleasure, in particular, is grounded on a pluralistic (or 'patchwork' or 'plural') approach to philosophy in general: 'He [Barthes] often resorts to a kind of philosophy vaguely labeled *pluralism*' (Barthes 1977: 69). 'Philosophically, it seems you are a materialist (if the word doesn't sound too old-fashioned); ethically, you divide yourself: as for the body, you are a hedonist; as for violence, you would rather be something of a Buddhist!' (Barthes 1977: 143). In short, Barthes believes that his work 'sum[s] up all the decadent philosophies: Epicureanism, eudaemonism, Asianism, Manichaeism, Pyrrhonism' (Barthes 1977: 144).

The ultimate statement of his philosophical pluralism perhaps comes in relation to sex:

> Who knows if this insistence on the plural is not a way of denying sexual duality. The opposition of the sexes must not be a law of Nature; therefore, the confrontations and paradigms must be dissolved, both the meanings and the sexes be pluralized: meaning will tend toward its multiplication, its dispersion (in the theory of the Text), and sex will be taken into no typology (there will be, for example, only *homosexualities*, whose plural will baffle any constituted, centered discourse, to the point where it seems to him virtually pointless to talk about it).
>
> (Barthes 1977: 69)

Pluralism (or, the *plural*) provides Barthes the opportunity not only to embrace all pleasure equally, but also to erase sexual duality and thereby embrace only *homosexualities*.

A boring hedonism

On September 17, 1979, less than a year before his untimely death on March 26, 1980, Barthes speaks of his boredom:

> A sort of despair came over me, I wanted to cry. I realized that I would have to give up boys, because they had no desire for me, and because I am either too scrupulous or too clumsy to impose mine on them; that this was an inescapable fact, proven by all my attempts at flirting, that this makes my life sad, that, ultimately, I'm bored, and that I must remove that interest, or that hope, from my life.
>
> (Barthes 2010: 171)

A few nights before (September 14, 1979), he speaks of being bored by some of the Pleynet painters at the opening of a museum ('the ones that bore me are the ones I know, the theoreticians, the sad ones [Devade, Cane, Dezeuze]') (Barthes 2010: 167). But boredom though is not just something that occupied him in later life.

In a letter to Philippe Rebeyrol on August 31, 1932, a 16-year-old Barthes describes himself as a 'decidedly boring fellow', who fears that he will 'bore' his friend (Barthes 2018: 2). This youthful boredom is again noted in *Barthes by Barthes*, where he says it goes back to his early youth:

> As a child, I was often and intensely bored. This evidently began very early, it has continued my whole life, in gusts (increasingly rare, it is true, thanks to work and to friends), and it has always been noticeable to others. A panic boredom, to the point of distress: like the kind I feel in panel discussions, lectures, parties among strangers, group amusements: wherever boredom can be seen. Might boredom be my form of hysteria?
>
> (Barthes 1977: 24)

Throughout *Barthes by Barthes* he discusses boredom in a variety of disparate contexts: avant-garde texts (Barthes 1977: 54); Michelet (Barthes 1977: 55); cruising ('Crazy, the power of distraction of a man who is bored, intimidated, or embarrassed by his work' [Barthes 1977: 71–72]); dreaming ('(nothing so boring as the account of a dream!)' [Barthes 1977: 87]); migraines (Barthes 1977: 124); self-commentary ('What a bore!' [Barthes 1977: 142]); foreseeable discourse (Barthes 1977: 149); scholarship 'apropos of Bataille' (Barthes 1977: 159); and postponement of books to be written (Barthes 1977: 174). Even the process of 'rereading' himself in *Barthes by Barthes* is found by Barthes to be boring (Barthes 1977: 71).

The presence of all of this boredom in the life of a self-professed hedonist should not be a major surprise, particularly to a writer who frequently places himself within the context of this 'very old tradition'. As noted earlier, boredom may philosophically be seen as either part of the life condition of the hedonist (a la Schopenhauer's *ennui*) or used as a criticism of hedonism as a way of life: an art of living. The fact that Barthes realises both that 'the art of living has no history' and that when pleasure vanishes it 'vanishes for good' (Barthes 1977: 50) should be a clue that the life of the Barthesian hedonist is a life *replete with boredom*. In short, the continual presence of boredom in the life of a person devoted to the pursuit of pleasure is almost proof of Barthes's lifelong commitment to hedonism—even if it was only later in life that he theorised—or dare we say, 'came out'—regarding this hedonism.

But why then, given all of the boredom in the life of this self-professed hedonist, does Barthes seem to be disappointed to hear that hedonism is regarded as a pessimism by Nietzsche ('for Nietzsche, hedonism is a pessimism')? Nietzsche surely derived this position from Schopenhauer, the great early influence in his philosophical life—and antagonist for the wide-ranging interest and debate about it in nineteenth-century Germany—and beyond. Again, Schopenhauer's pessimism regards the hedonistic life as one *characterised by* restlessness, boredom (*ennui*), and, ultimately, suffering. Does Barthes really expect us to embrace hedonism as an *optimism*? Is this the project of morality that he is pursuing under the intertext of our parenthetical Nietzsche?

My thesis here is that the *non-parenthetical* intertext for Barthes's hedonism is *not* Nietzsche (hence the parentheses for him). But it is also not the usual hedonistic suspects he lines up in *The Pleasure of the Text* and *Barthes by Barthes*: Epicurus, Diderot, Sade, and Fourier. Nor is it any of the decadent philosophies he mentions (though rarely discusses): Epicureanism, eudaemonism, Asianism, Manichaeism, and Pyrrhonism. Rather, the intertext for Barthes's hedonism is the moral philosophy of André Gide. Thus, the parenthetical citations of Nietzsche, Gide, and the 'desire to write' serve to connect them all with the genre of 'morality', or more particularly, *Gidean* morality.

A sickly morality

André Gide sparked in Roland Barthes the desire both to write—and to become a hedonist, that is to say, a moral philosopher. Gide also influenced Barthes's fragmentary writing style (which could mistakenly also be associated with Nietzsche's fragmentary writing style):

> His first, or nearly first text (1942) consists of fragments; this choice is then justified in the Gidean manner 'because incoherence is preferable to a distorting order'. Since then, as a matter of fact, he has never stopped writing in brief bursts: the brief scenes of *Mythologies*, the articles and prefaces of *Critical Essays*, the lexias of *S/Z*, the fragments of the second essay on Sade in *Sade, Fourier, Loyola* and of *The Pleasure of the Text*.
>
> (Barthes 1977: 93)

But Gide represents more than just a style of writing for Barthes—he is literally his *Abgrund*:

> One of his first articles (1942) concerned Gide's *Journal;* the writing of another (*'En Grèce',* 1944) was evidently imitated from *Les nourritures terrestres.* And Gide occupied a great place in his early reading: a diagonal cross-breed of Alsace and Gascony, as Gide was of Normandy and Languedoc, Protestant, having a taste for 'letters' and fond of playing the piano, without counting the rest—how could he have failed to recognize himself, to desire himself in this writer? The Gidean *Abgrund*, the Gidean core, unchanging, still forms in my head a stubborn swarm. Gide is my original language, my *Ursuppe*, my literary soup.
>
> (Barthes 1977: 99)

Going back to his 1942 essay on Gide, 'On Gide and His Journal', we learn a bit more about Barthes early attraction to this writer. Here he calls Gide 'another Montaigne' (Barthes 1982: 3), presumably because both are sceptics who question all values, and both revel in their uncertainties and inconsistencies. He also places Gide and Nietzsche (along with another thinker) together in rarified company:

> In the last hundred years, there have been three men who have had the most intense, the most intimate, and even what I call the most fraternal attraction to Christ's person—outside of dogmatic or mystical knowledge: Nietzsche (as a *frère ennemi*), Rozanov, and Gide.
>
> (Barthes 1982: 9–10)

In the case of Gide, this fraternal attraction to Christ's person leads to the somewhat odd combination of evangelical spirit coupled with hedonism (Bruckner 2006: 243). Both Gide and Nietzsche are also linked by their break from conventional morality in their work. For Gide, a trip to North Africa in 1893 and 1894 brought him into contact with the radically different moral standards of the Arab world that helped liberate him from Victorian conventions. This intellectual revolt also brought Gide to a growing awareness of his homosexuality, where he was aided by a famous literary mentor, Oscar Wilde.

In 1897, Gide published *The Fruits of the Earth* (*Les nourritures terrestres*), a book-length prose poem, where he established a sophisticated hedonism, which both glorifies pleasure and apologises for detachment. However, for Gide, the most important thing in life was 'not satisfying hunger or slaking thirst, but sustaining a mood of exhilaration' (Bruckner 2006: 243). Moreover, according to Pascal Bruckner, Gide believed that the

> noble desire of desiring is always to be preferred to a grim satisfaction: 'Possession seemed to me less valuable than pursuit, and I came more and more to prefer thirst to quenching it, the promise of pleasure to pleasure itself'.
>
> (Bruckner 2006: 243)

As such, Gidean hedonism, which places a higher value on the pursuit of pleasure, differs greatly from Barthes's hedonism, where quenching pleasure—albeit a wide spectrum of pleasures—is clearly preferable.

The next major step in Gide's revolt from his puritan, moralistic upbringing was his first novel (or as he termed it, *récit*), *The Immoralist* (*L'immoraliste*), which was written in 1901 and published in 1902. In *The Immoralist*, Michel marries a family friend, Marceline, to cheer up his dying father and provide for his own needs. While recovering from tuberculosis in North Africa, Michel finds himself drawn sexually to young Arab boys. He is encouraged by a friend in France to ignore moral convention and pursue his desires. However, as he is pursuing his desires, he is also ignoring the needs of his pregnant wife who has contracted tuberculosis. She has a miscarriage and later dies in the presence of Michel. The work is a moral examination of hedonism as well as a critique of *The Fruits of the Earth* in that it explores the point where pursuit of individual pleasure (*hedonism*) must be superseded by altruistic concerns, that is, care for others (or, *altruistic hedonism*).

In his essay, Barthes connects the self-examination of Gide's journal to his novels and *récits*. 'It is because at a certain moment he [Gide] wanted to be someone that he summoned up … Michel', comments Barthes, 'that he wrote *Fruits of the Earth*, *The Immoralist*, and *The*

Counterfeiters' (Barthes 1982: 12). This is then followed by a quote from a Gide journal entry from 1924: 'The desire to portray characters one has encountered is, I believe, quite common. But the creation of new characters becomes a natural need only in those tormented by an imperious complexity and whom their own gesture does not exhaust' (Barthes 1982: 12). In short, Barthes views works such as *Fruits of the Earth* and *The Immoralist* as Gide 'should be':

> If we admit that the work is an expression of Gide's will (Lafcadio's life, Michel's, Edouard's), the *Journal* is actually the converse of the work, its contrary complement. The work: Gide as he should (would) be. The *Journal*: Gide as he is, or more exactly: as Eduoard, Michel, and Lafcadio have made him.
>
> (Barthes 1982: 12)

Barthes views récits such as *The Immoralist* as 'fictionalizations—if that—of a case, of a theme, of a pathology' (Barthes 1982: 12–13). They are also 'myths' wherein

> Each hero engages the reader, promulgates example or iconoclasm. Mythology, as in these récits of Gide's, proves nothing: it is a fine work of art in which a great deal of faith circulates; a fine fiction in which one agrees to believe because it explains life and at the same time is a little stronger, a little larger than life (it affords the image of an ideal; every mythology is a dream). And these récits of Gide's, like every myth, are an equivalence between an abstract reality and a concrete fiction. All of these books are Christian works.
>
> (Barthes 1982: 13)

Gide's work can be described as grounded in 'never resolved tensions between a strict artistic discipline, a puritanical moralism, and the desire for unlimited sensual indulgence and abandonment of life' (Frenz 1969: 428). These are the words the Nobel Prize organisation used in 1947 when it announced his award for literature. He wrote plays, novels, journals, letters, poems, and critiques as well as did translations. Barthes writes that it comprises 'a net of which no mesh can be dropped' and that it is futile to try to divide it up chronologically or methodologically (Barthes 1982: 11). 'It almost requires to be read in the fashion of certain Bibles', comments Barthes (1982: 11). Is it much of a jump then to regard Gide as Barthes's 'Bible' on hedonism, rather than say Sade or Fourier, the two writers he refers to most frequently in reference to hedonism?

Barthes says that Gide possesses 'a conscience which ordinary morality has the odd habit of calling sickly' (Barthes 1982: 8). Indeed, Gide's moral philosophy meets with a mixed reception which alternately calls him a liberator, a corrupter of youth, an immoral man, and a literary moralist—or, more recently, a 'homosexual moralist' (Kogan 2006; Pollard 1991). But Barthes defends Gide's moral consciousness because he 'explains himself, surrenders himself, delicately retracts or asserts himself bravely enough, but never abuses the reader as to his mutations' (Barthes 1982: 8). For him, Gide puts 'everything in the *movement* of his thought and not in its brutal profession' (Barthes 1982: 8). Might not the same be said of Barthes? Particularly of his final movement and mutation to hedonist?

Gide does these things, according to Barthes, out of authenticity (the impulses of a soul are the mark of its authenticity), aesthetic pleasure, the scrupulous search for truth, and, 'lastly, the moral importance accorded to states of conflict, perhaps because they are warrants of humility' (Barthes 1982: 8). As the moral philosophy of Gide is where Barthes started his journey as a writer, what prevents us now explaining his late turn to hedonism, or, alternately, to the genre of morality, as a return to his beginnings? After all, as we saw, Barthes adores 'beginnings'. Jonathan Culler comments that 'Barthes's revival of hedonism may be his most difficult project to assess, for it seems to indulge in some of the mystifications he had effectively exposed, yet it continues to challenge intellectual orthodoxy' (Culler 2002: 84). I would wager, reading Barthes's revival through his formative and lasting affection for the work on Gide makes this process a whole lot easier to assess.

Conclusion

Barthes's revival of hedonism was not an exercise in academic philosophy even if he seeks to place himself within the context of its 'repressed' traditions. Rather, it was in practice a journey back to how he came to be a writer concerned with not just the art of writing, but also the art of living. Gide appears to have been his constant companion in this journey from his earliest days as a writer to his final assessments of his career in *Barthes by Barthes*. When Barthes speaks of 'actually' seeing Gide eating a pear and reading a book, it is in contradistinction to the way he 'imagined' him: '(the way I imagined Gide travelling from Russia to the Congo, reading his classics and writing his notebooks in the dining car, waiting for the meals to be served …)' (Barthes 1977: 77). The major difference between Barthes's 'actual' Gide and his 'imagined' one comes down to a pear. The same fruit the Augustine made into the symbol of moral guilt and disobedience in his *Confessions*.

For me, this is the most revealing moment in Barthes's account of his hedonism. And it comes in the context of a fragment entitled 'The writer as fantasy' (*L'écrivain comme fantasme*). 'Surely', writes Barthes, 'there is no longer a single adolescent who has this fantasy: *to be a writer!*' (Barthes 1977: 77). 'Imagine', he continues, 'wanting to copy not the works but the practices of any contemporary—his way of strolling through the world, a notebook in his pocket and a phrase in his head' (Barthes 1977: 77). Barthes is speaking here not about the 'art of writing', viz., copying works, but rather the 'art of life', viz., copying *life practices*. This line is then followed by his picture of the two Gides: one imagined and one actual. The fragment then concludes as follows: 'For what the fantasy imposes is the writer as we can see him in his private diary, *the writer minus his work*: supreme form of the sacred: the mark and the void' (Barthes 1977: 79). Who was the Gide we see in his journal? For that matter, who was the Barthes we see in *his* private diary? We got a glimpse of this Barthes (of his private diary) above in the selection from *Incidents*; for Gide, his journal was the place where he could 'revel in his contradictions', where 'I am never', rather 'I become' (Kogan 2006: 537)—the place where Gide is the *existential* hedonist.

Unlike Gide, who started publishing selections of his journals during his lifetime (in 1932, to be specific), making him the first author to do this, Barthes's private writing remained private until after his death, when some of it started to be released. Still, writes Barthes, 'Am I not justified in considering everything I have written as a clandestine and stubborn effort to bring to light again, someday, quite freely, the theme of the Gidean "journal"?'—given that 'the (autobiographical) "journal" is, nowadays, discredited' (Barthes 1977: 95). The spectacle though of a young person fantasising about revealing their private writings to the world is a peculiar one to resist, that is, to use as the basis of rejecting the fantasy of becoming a writer. Perhaps it is because in such journals and diaries, the art of living is revealed in ways that an author's work cannot match in terms of authenticity. Or, more specifically, in the case of a philosopher such as Barthes, in terms of *parrēsia*, the ability it gives him to speak the truth freely. The full scope of Barthes's hedonism is not possible without *parrēsia*. So too is his ability to pursue the art of living in the spirit of his ancient Greek philosophical predecessors, the hedonists who he at times seems to be so interested in associating with in his work. Nevertheless, based on his fragment, 'The writer as fantasy', the prospect of being seen in his private diary makes the potential young writer tremble with the prospect of this as a career. Hence, Gide's pear, or, a hedonism with extreme existential guilt. If for Nietzsche, hedonism is a pessimism, then for Barthes, hedonism without boredom is only a fantasy—that one can live out in a private diary.

In conclusion, Barthes's hedonism as *art de textualité* famously distinguishes between the *plaisir* of Readerly textual fulfilment and the *jouissance* of Writerly textual unsettlement. There is also the textual pleasure that comes from finding ecstatic moments in Readerly texts. Of these three forms of pleasure, literary criticism and theory have tended to focus its attention on this last one because of the way it offers a kind of higher resolution of the difference between the comfort of *plaisir* and the discomfort of *jouissance*. However, when Barthes's hedonism as *art de textualité* is regarded within the context of the debate between the comfort provided by the products of the happiness industry and the discomfort of the theoretical critique of happiness, one might take the opportunity to see in his distinction among 'pleasures' a kind of higher resolution of the debates discussed in the first two chapters of this book. In hedonism as *art de textualité*, the status of literature is broadened to include both literature as product of the happiness industry *and* literature as critique of happiness—as well as Writerly literature as the embodiment of hedonism.

But if this were the only conclusion of Barthes's hedonism, then it might be argued that it is merely a return to the textualism of late twentieth-century literary theory, rather than a forward-looking response early twenty-first century debates on happiness. It is at this point that Barthes's hedonism as *art de vivre* might be viewed as moving beyond the arid structuralist/poststructuralist debates regarding textuality to nascent biopolitical concerns regarding life and ways of living. It is already well established and widely appreciated that Barthes's hedonism allows for pleasure in a wide range of texts. However, what is less recognised is Barthes the moralist and moral philosopher who is concerned with the art of living—or, dare we say, living *truly*?

Barthes's hedonism as *art de vivre* reveals his struggles with boredom to be a lifelong concern manifested by his sense of morality. To regard Barthes as a moralist is both to locate a figure in the history of philosophy able to overcome the alleged 'pessimism' and 'boredom' of hedonism by coordinating the dual arts of textuality and living. Moreover, and perhaps more importantly, Barthes's hedonism provides a robustness to the stature of literature by emphasising an overdetermined sense of pleasure—one that includes as key components the pleasures of both money and sex. Barthes's hedonism offers a grand path towards resolving the Janus-faced standing of literature with respect to happiness in the new millennium, wherein one direction looks towards embracing happiness in literature and the other looks towards overcoming it. Moreover, unlike Žižek who rejects hedonism, Barthes shows us a way to fully accept it as a way of living albeit not as the *spiritualised* pursuit of pleasure, but rather as an *aesthetic* hedonism.

Notes

1 The Aristippus translation in the Loeb edition of Diogenes Laertius is as follows: 'Being asked what he had gained from philosophy, he replied, "The ability to feel at ease in any society"' (Laertius 1925: 197).
2 In support of this parallel process of meditation taken on by Barthes, consider Edmund Husserl's comment that Descartes' *Meditations* 'are not intended to be a merely private concern of the philosopher Descartes … . Rather they draw the prototype for any beginning philosopher's necessary meditations, the meditations out of which alone a philosophy can grow originally' (1960: 2).

4 Real happiness is revolutionary

Badiou, antiphilosophy, and the metaphysics of happiness from Spinoza and Pascal to Mallarmé and Beckett

The hedonism of Roland Barthes gives the art of writing and the art of living a new meaning. He also provides a pathway to *parrēsia*, which was one of the concerns of Lacan and Žižek concerning the pursuit of happiness. But while aesthetic hedonism may offer a path to happiness, it is also one continuously threatened by boredom. There is only so much dancing and singing one can do *à la* Pharrell regarding Barthes's hedonism before boredom inevitably sets in to darken our lives. Fortunately though there is another path to happiness *and* truth. It requires though that we go back to Žižek's comment that happiness is *not* the truth, but rather a 'category of mere Being' (Žižek 2002: 59). But what does this mean? Or, more importantly, what *can* this mean in the pursuit of *real* happiness?

Žižek illustrates this claim by describing a time when the people of Czechoslovakia were 'in a way' happy. It occurred because 'three fundamental conditions of happiness were fulfilled': first, their basic material needs were satisfied; second, there was something to be blamed for everything that went wrong—this was the Other, which in the case of Czechoslovakia was 'the Party'; and third, there was an Other Place to dream about, which here was the consumerist West. But according to desire, the fragile balance of happiness in this country was disturbed by desire—a desire to go beyond the fragile conditions of their happiness to a system where the majority of people are now less happy (Žižek 2002: 58–59). In short, the desire for something more destroyed their short-lived happiness.

As we saw earlier, Žižek and the psychoanalytic tradition will have nothing to do with happiness. These particular comments by Žižek about happiness were published a year after September 11 and were intended as remarks about happiness after these tragic events. Happiness as a category of mere being is something that was said to be 'confused, indeterminate, inconsistent (take the proverbial answer of

DOI: 10.4324/9781003178941-5

a German immigrant to the USA who, asked: "Are you happy?", answered: "Yes, yes, I am very happy, *aber glücklich bin ich nicht* ...")' (Žižek 2002: 59). For those whose German is rusty, the joke here about the 'inconsistency' of happiness comes by knowing that the German translates as 'but luckily I am not'.

Rather than go alone in stating happiness as a category of mere Being, and, as such, confused, indeterminate, and inconsistent, Žižek says that these are 'Alain Badiou's terms'. However, when Žižek revises this passage nearly two decades later for a chapter in his book *A Left that Dares Speak its Name*, 'Badiou's terms' is changed to 'as Hegel would have put it' (Žižek 2020: 248). Why the change? Presumably because Badiou subsequently argued that we should not give up on the aspiration to be happy. Rather, for Badiou, all philosophy is a metaphysics of happiness, and that in order to be truly happy, we need philosophy. Badiou's position here is thus clearly at odds with Žižek's, which concludes that we must give up on the aspiration to be happy.

Badiou has commented on happiness in a many different places over the years. However, he most completely develops his position on it in a book entitled *The Metaphysics of Real Happiness*. It is an important study because not only does it provide an extended account of the 'being' of happiness, that is, its ontology, but also because it bestows happiness with revolutionary potential. In the context of this study, it is a position on happiness that avoids both the pitfalls of the happiness industry as well as the impossibilities for happiness that stem from the psychoanalytic position. Moreover, unlike Barthes, whose happiness is located primarily in acts of morality linked to the arts of textuality and living, Badiou's happiness is one that is encountered in *philosophical* acts. As we shall see, it finds poetic inspiration in Stéphane Mallarmé, its literary correlate in the fiction of Samuel Beckett, and a philosophical precursor in the rationalist metaphysics of Baruch Spinoza.

Tumbling dice

'Philosophy', writes Alain Badiou, 'is not a matter of life or of happiness'. 'But neither', he continues, 'is it a matter death or unhappiness'. 'We will live or die in any case, on top of it all, and as for being happy or unhappy, it is what we are constantly required not to care about—neither for the other nor for ourselves' (Badiou 2012: 35).

These comments were made by Badiou 30 years ago in an essay he published on his changing attitude towards his 'absolute master', Jean-Paul Sartre (Badiou 1990). They are intended to show one aspect of his continuing solidarity with Sartre, namely his 'determining "existential" motif' (Badiou 2012: 35). But aside from revealing the continuing importance of Sartre to Badiou, the essay is also significant because it reveals some continuing aspects of the latter's general approach to happiness—ones that he will develop in much more detail many years later.

Badiou illustrates his point about Sartre's existential motif by citing Mallarmé's poem *A Throw of the Dice* (*Un Coup de Dés*). This poem was first published in a journal in May of 1897 but did not appear on its own until 1914. Mallarmé corrected the proofs of a deluxe edition of the poem in 1898 but died the same year and the edition never appeared. This deluxe edition, which would include illustrations, was to have unusually large dimensions, measuring approximately eleven-and-one-half inches in width and fifteen-and-one-half inches in height. The dimensions were due to the physical layout of the poem that includes varying font sizes and many white space or 'blanks'. *A Throw of the Dice* is stylistically innovative and occupies a special place in both Mallarmé's oeuvre and European literature (Weinfield 1994: 264–265). It is also important to understanding Badiou's notion of happiness.

A Throw of the Dice attempts 'to establish meaning in an essentially meaningless universe', writes one commentator (Weinfield 1994: 266). But it does so in the same way that Pablo Picasso's *Les Demoiselles d'Avignon* (1907) would a decade later: by exploding the linearity of perception. Writes another commentator,

> the poem decentres into constellations of words, scattered in a disorderly fashion in the four corners, edges and even in the folds of eleven large double pages on which this poem sprawls like an archipelago in some kind of typological game of capitals, italics and bold lettering that prevents a cursive and purely rational reading of the work.
>
> (Marty 2018: n.p.)

While there are stanzas and rhymes, they are hidden in the verbal shipwreck of the poem—a shipwreck that is actually the theme of the poem, 'one in which both the poet and poetry drown: no verse, no throw of the dice, can ever succeed in attesting that beauty is something other than fortuitous, other than the fruit of chance' (Marty 2018: n.p.). But the stylistic innovation goes even deeper as the poem functions like a hall of mirrors: not only are the first and last words of the poem the same ('A Throw of the Dice') but among other mirroring techniques is the use of the word 'chance' itself, which in Arabic is *al-zhar*, which literally means a throw of the dice (Marty 2018: n.p.).

Most importantly, though, the universe created by Mallarmé through the typographical cosmos of this poem is one where the gods are no longer present. Therefore, they have no role in transcendentally conferring meaning on the universe. Pascal, who was noted earlier as one of the foremost pessimists regarding happiness, is the most explicit forerunner to Mallarmé's poem. The motif of the 'dice throw' goes back to Pascal's Wager, where he uses his reason to prepare the way for faith in God.

For Pascal, there is no rational proof for or against the existence of God. 'If there is a God', says Pascal, 'He is infinitely incomprehensible, since, having neither parts nor limits, He has no affinity to us' (Pascal 1932: 66). However, while reason cannot prove or disprove God's existence, it does tell us that we are involved in a wager when we choose to believe or not believe in God: By believing or not believing in God, we are wagering that he exists or does not exist. 'Your reason is no more shocking in choosing one rather than the other, since you must of necessity choose', comments Pascal (1932: 67). If you wager that God exists, and he does exist, the payoff is eternal happiness and immortality; if you wager that God exists, and he doesn't exist, you lose nothing; if you wager that God doesn't exist, and he does, an eternity of damnation awaits; if you wager that God doesn't exist, and he doesn't, you lose nothing. Consider then the wager that God exists: When 'you gain, you gain all; if you lose, you lose nothing' (Pascal 1932: 67). 'Wager, then', concludes Pascal, 'without hesitation that He is' (Pascal 1932: 67). This wager was addressed to Pascal's sceptical and freethinking friends, some of whom enjoyed gambling.

Pascal, in addition to being a philosopher, was also a mathematical genius, who made important contributions to number theory, probability theory, and physics. His wager turns considerations of 'an eternity of life and happiness' from a merely speculative endeavour into a mathematical decision regarding infinity. Writes Pascal,

> if there were an infinity of chances, of which one only would be for you, you would still be right in wagering one to win two, and you would act stupidly, being obliged to play, by refusing to stake one life against three at a game in which out of an infinity of chances there is one for you, if there were an infinity of happy life to gain. But there is here an infinity of happy life to gain, a chance of gain against a finite number of chances of loss, and what you stake is finite.
>
> (Pascal 1932: 67)

In the hands of Mallarmé, though, Pascal's Wager regarding infinite happiness is re-enacted in an environment where God is dead. 'If God is dead (and Sartre convinced me of this more than Nietzsche, who was too concerned with disentangling himself from the Nazarene)', writes Badiou, 'this does not mean that everything is possible—and even less that nothing is' (Badiou 2012: 34). 'It means', continues Badiou, 'that there is precisely nothing better, nothing greater, nothing truer, than the answers of which we are capable' (Badiou 2012: 34).

Badiou says that the figure of Mallarmé literally haunted Sartre, who even devoted an entire book to him where he describes him as 'the poet of nothingness' (Badiou 2012: 29). But still, for Badiou, what Sartre fails to see in Mallarmé is 'the *affirmative* capacity of the poet's thinking' (Badiou 2012: 29). 'I saw in Mallarmé's poems and prose', comments Badiou, 'the most radical effort ever conducted to *think thinking*' (Badiou 2012: 30). Moreover, he saw in Mallarmé a poet whose thoughts were 'symmetrical to mathematics' (Badiou 2012: 29), a passion that Badiou shares with Pascal—and somewhat further back, with Plato, who Badiou says 'to whom I constantly return with a quiet remorse, because of the degree to which the "objective" ideality and much-flaunted primacy of essence over existence seemed to contradict the Sartrean doctrinal body' (Badiou 2012: 30).

For Badiou, the point of Mallarmé's *A Throw of the Dice* 'is to throw the dice, at least once, if possible' (Badiou 2012: 35). But the old man in Mallarmé's poem, comments Badiou, 'does not come to this resolution easily' (Badiou 2012: 35). Rather, says Badiou quoting Mallarmé, he 'hesitates corpse by the arm separated from the secret it withholds rather than play as a hoary maniac the game in the name of the waves' (Badiou 2012: 29; quoting Mallarmé 1994: 130). For Badiou, drawing upon Mallarmé's *A Throw of the Dice*, happiness—as well as life and many other matters—is this 'hesitation to play the part in the name of the waves' (Badiou 2012: 36). Pascal's 'eternal' life in the Wager becomes in the hands of Mallarmé and Badiou's dice throw living '*forever* as "a corpse cut off by its arm from the secret it withholds"' (Badiou 2012: 36). It is a life and happiness that for Mallarmé and Badiou that

> is resolved in the disjunction between a corpse and a secret. Every human being holds a possible pass for at least one truth. Such is its secret, which our common lot under the law of Capital turns into the other extreme of a cadaver.
>
> (Badiou 2012: 36)

Badiou then brings this radical disjunction between a corpse and a secret to bear on thought and thinking. For him, what the tale of the old man in Mallarmé's poem reveals is that if 'every thought emits a throw of the dice', then we must conclude that 'where there are no dice throws, there also is no thought' (Badiou 2012: 36). For Badiou, this is the 'unconditional demand' of the wager—albeit one that is conducted *without God* (Badiou 2012: 36). Thus, concludes Badiou:

> All humans are capable of thought, all humans are aleatorically summoned to exist as subjects. And if all humans are capable of thought, the guideline is clear: throw the dice, play the part in the name of the waves, and then be faithful to this throw, which is not so difficult, once thrown, the dice come back to you as Constellation. This Constellation is said [by Mallarmé's *A Throw of the Dice* to be] 'cold with neglect and disuse [*désuétude*]', but why should philosophy have to promise that the truth keep us warm and fuzzy, that it be convivial and affective?
>
> (Badiou 2012: 36)

The Constellation Badiou is referring to is the one created in *A Throw of the Dice*, which Mallarmé describes in the penultimate line as

> A CONSTELLATION cold from forgetfulness and desuetude not so much that it doesn't number on some vacant and superior surface the successive shock in the ways of stars of a total account in the making keeping vigil doubting rolling shining and meditating before coming to a halt at some terminus that sacrifices it.
>
> (Mallarmé 1994: 144)

Mallarmé's final line, 'All Thought emits a Throw of the Dice' (Mallarmé 1994: 144), reinforces the special nature of thought commented upon by Badiou above.

These reflections on Mallarmé's *A Throw of the Dice* are revisited 25 years later as Badiou's opening salvo in his major study of happiness. He tells us that the last line of Mallarmé's poem is an 'enigmatic formula [that] applies equally to philosophy' (Badiou 2019: 42). Writes Badiou,

> The fundamental desire of philosophy is to think and realize the universal, among other things because a happiness that is not universal, which excludes the possibility of being shared by every other human animal capable of becoming its subject, is not a real happiness.
>
> (Badiou 2019: 42)

Nevertheless, this fundamental desire of philosophy is like the throw of the dice in Mallarmé's poem: there is hesitation as it is not the result of necessity. 'It exists in a movement', writes Badiou, 'that is always a wager, a risky engagement'. Moreover, as an engagement of thought, the fundamental desire of philosophy is indelibly marked by chance.

For Badiou, from the poetry of Mallarmé, we come to conclusion that philosophy, particularly as it orients itself towards the universality of happiness, can be characterised as having four fundamental dimensions of desire: revolt, logic, universality, and risk. Each of these dimensions, though, finds in the Western world 'strong negative pressure' (Badiou 2019: 43). Or, as Badiou puts it, the Western world is 'inappropriate' for revolt, logic, universality, and risk. But why? In the case of revolt, it is inappropriate because the world is already regarded as one in which freedom reigns. Therefore, there is nothing better that could be wanted or hoped for than a free world (Badiou 2019: 43). In the case of logic, this world is inappropriate because it is 'submitted to the illogical dimension of communication', in which words, statements, and images are transmitted on the principle of incoherence (Badiou 2019: 44). In the case of universality, this world is inappropriate both because the material form of its universality is monetary abstraction and because it is specialised and fragmentary. For Badiou, this monetary material form of the universal and the fragmented and specialised character of this world puts extreme pressure on the universal (Badiou 2019: 44–45). And finally, this world is inappropriate for risk or wager because it is one where no one 'any longer has the means to deliver their existence to chance' (Badiou 2019: 45). Consequently, these four things become 'obstacles' that 'reduce the ineluctable idea of the true life, of happiness, to the semblance of consumer satisfaction' (Badiou 2019: 46) which of course is something we discussed earlier in the context of the influence of Watson's behavioural psychology on marketing and advertising.

But these are not the only obstacles to real happiness: so too are the three principal currents in philosophy—the phenomenological and hermeneutical (e.g., Martin Heidegger and Hans-Georg Gadamer); the analytical (e.g., Ludwig Wittgenstein, Rudolf Carnap, and contemporary American and British analytic philosophy); and the postmodern (e.g. Jacques Derrida and Jean-François Lyotard) (Badiou 2019: 46–47). What is shared by these three currents is the announcement of 'the end of metaphysics, and therefore, in some way, the end of philosophy itself, at least in its classical sense or, as

Heidegger would say, in its destinal sense' (Badiou 2019: 49). Thus, Badiou proposes that we

> break with these frames of thought, to rediscover or constitute in renewed configurations a style of philosophical path that is not that of interpretation [viz., phenomenology and hermeneutics], nor that of grammarian analysis [viz., analytical philosophy], nor that of edges, equivocations and deconstructions [viz., postmodern philosophy].
> (Badiou 2019: 56)

So if these three major currents of philosophy present obstacles to true happiness, what style of philosophy does not? Answer: the philosophical style Badiou employed in what he calls 'my great philosophical treatises: *Being and Event* and *Logics of Worlds*, or in any case their outlines, *Manifesto for Philosophy* and *Second Manifesto for Philosophy*' (Badiou 2019: 56).

He describes the style of these works as a rediscovered 'foundational, decisive philosophical style' with affinities, for example, with the philosophical style of Descartes (Badiou 2019: 56). Herein, there will be at least two dominant themes: first, 'language is not the absolute horizon of thought', and second, 'the proper, irreducible, singular role of philosophy is to establish a fixed point in discourse' (Badiou 2019: 57). Both of these themes are counter to both the linguistic turn in philosophy (viz., analytic philosophy) and literary theory (viz., postmodern, or better, poststructuralist literary theory). As such, the quest for true happiness that began with Mallarmé's tumbling dice results in Badiou's proclamation that 'philosophy is sick' (Badiou 2019: 65). 'The contemporary world has more need of philosophy than philosophy itself believes', comments Badiou. But not the philosophy offered by its major current. Rather, the contemporary world needs Badiou's style of philosophy—in the same way that the turn of the century needed the stylistic revolutions of Mallarmé (in poetry) and Picasso (in art). It is a philosophy he describes as a 'logical revolt' that combines a desire for revolution (as 'real happiness [demands] that one rise up against the world as it is and against the dictatorship of established opinions' [Badiou 2019: 41]) *and* 'a rational exigency' (because revolution alone is 'incapable of achieving the goals it sets [for] itself' (Badiou 2019: 41).

The critique of happiness

Badiou holds philosophy accountable to happiness. In fact, if done appropriately, philosophy and philosophy alone—as we will see—holds the potential for real happiness. However, philosophical currents such as phenomenology and hermeneutics, analytic philosophy, and the so-called postmodern philosophy are *not* accountable because their calls for the end of metaphysics make real happiness philosophically impossible. This puts academic philosophy into a difficult position: either accept metaphysics into your philosophical current on the terms Badiou provides *or* provide no welcoming place in your philosophy for real happiness. Viewed from this perspective, the stakes of Badiou's quarrel with phenomenology and hermeneutics, analytic philosophy, and so-called postmodern philosophy is nothing less than one about the source of real happiness in our world—something regarded by many in the philosophical tradition as the goal of life.

Still, in spite of Badiou's quarrel with academic philosophy, the critique and rejection of happiness is not a central part of the operating system of academic philosophy. In other words, happiness may have a role in it, but the functioning of the system in no way depends on it. However, the *critique* of happiness *is* the hallmark of philosophy's other: what Badiou terms *antiphilosophy*. For Badiou, an antiphilosopher is someone who 'opposes the drama of his existence to conceptual constructions, for whom truth exists, absolutely, but must be encountered, experienced, rather than thought or constructed' (Badiou 2019: 67). Some of the key philosophers who fulfil these conditions argues Badiou are Pascal, Rousseau, Kierkegaard, Nietzsche, Wittgenstein, and Lacan. Moreover, each of them—albeit in a different way and to different extremes—takes part in a critique of happiness.

What is interesting about these antiphilosophers is that Badiou is both drawn to their work and pushed away from it. For example, in the case of Pascal, we saw how his wager is important to Badiou's philosophy. Nevertheless, without God it is not *Pascal's* Wager, but rather *Mallarme's*. 'The philosopher that I am', writes Badiou, 'conceptual, systematic, infatuated by the matheme—can evidently not cede to the song of these marvellous and carnivorous sirens that are the antiphilosophers' (Badiou 2019: 68). Nevertheless, Badiou is still drawn to their work:

> What impassions me, in these violent and superb adversaries, is the following: against the contractual and deliberative moderation inflicted upon us today as a norm, they recall that the subject has no chance to hold itself at the height of the Absolute except in the tense and paradoxical element of choice. One must wager, says Pascal; one must encounter in oneself, says Rousseau, the voice of conscience; and Kierkegaard, 'through the choice, [the subject]

> submerges itself in that which is being chosen, and when it does not choose, it withers away'. And, in regard to real happiness, it is subordinated to the chancy encounters which summon us to choose. It is here that the true life appears, or, if we weaken, disappears, hardly glimpsed.
>
> (Badiou 2019: 69)

For Badiou, as antiphilosophers, none of these thinkers should be regarded as proponents of relativism, scepticism, democracy, cultural diversity, or the 'variegation of opinions' (Badiou 2019: 67). Rather, they are all 'the hardest, most intolerant of believers' (Badiou 2019: 67). Moreover, as a group, they have the severe opinions of philosophers that do not practice their brand of 'antiphilosophy'. For example, Badiou says that Rousseau calls Voltaire, Diderot, and Hume 'corrupt, conspirers', and Nietzsche says the philosopher is the '"criminal of criminals", to be shot without delay' (Badiou 2019: 68).

Badiou's line in the sand of philosophical history is important to acknowledge because it is also an *unlikely* line regarding potential philosophical sources of real encounter with happiness. To be sure, most look to Pascal, Kierkegaard, and Nietzsche as masters of a critique of happiness. One of the special features, though, of Badiou's philosophy is that he finds something affirmative and important in their work that contributes to his account of real happiness. For example, he argues that these antiphilosophers 'help us to elude the traps of consent' that are a regular feature of globalisation and modernisation.

'Everyday it is explained to us', comments Badiou, 'that the constraints of globalization and modernization, not counting the immutable rules of user-friendly democracy, reasonably oblige us to consent to this or that' (Badiou 2019: 72). Antiphilosophers such as Kierkegaard avoid the consent traps of globalisation and modernisation by allowing us to choose even if it is only despair that we end up choosing. 'Even if, as Kierkegaard states', writes Badiou, '"in choosing in the absolute sense," that is, against the injunction of the reasonable and the legal, "I choose despair", it nevertheless remains the case that "in despair I choose the Absolute, because I myself am the absolute"'. For Badiou, 'this is why, for the great tormented beings who are the antiphilosophers, happiness is not made for jovial guys—a certain dose of despair is the condition of real happiness' (Badiou 2019: 72). Thus in many ways despair functions in relation to happiness in Badiou as boredom functions in relation to hedonism in Barthes: for both these things are necessary albeit unfortunate side effects.

In sum, the lesson regarding *real* happiness that Badiou gleans from the antiphilosophical critiques of happiness can be summed up as follows: 'If you want to become something other than [what] you are ordained to be, have confidence only in encounters, devote your fidelity to what is officially prohibited, keep yourself on the roads of the impossible' (Badiou 2019: 74). The lesson of finding ways to 're-route' ourselves in a globalised and modern world that at every corner works to trap us into consenting to things or ways of being we do not want is epitomised for Badiou in the literature of Beckett.

One of Beckett's characters who illustrates the re-routing of happiness described by Badiou is the 'old so dying woman' from of *Ill Seen Ill Said* (Beckett 2010: 456). Published in 1981, when Beckett himself was 75 years of age, it depicts a woman who appears to be alone in a cabin. She is lying in a state between life and death, which Beckett describes as 'So dead'. This dying old woman lies watching her memories 'In the madhouse of the skull and nowhere else' (Beckett 2010: 456). Writes Beckett,

> From where she lies she sees Venus rise. On. From where she lies when the skies are clear she sees Venus rise following the sun. Then she rails at the source of all life. On. At evening when the skies are clear she savours its star's revenge. At the other window. Right upright on her old chair she watches for the radiant one. Her old deal spindlebacked kitchen chair. It emerges from out the last rays and sinking ever brighter is engulfed in its turn. On. She sits on erect and rigid in the deepening gloom. Such helplessness to move she cannot help. Heading on foot for a particular point often she freezes on the way. Unable till long after to move on not knowing wither or for what purpose. Down on her knees especially she finds it hard not to remain so forever. Hand resting on hand on some convenient support. Such as the foot of her bed. And on them her head. There then she sits as though turned to stone face to the night. Save for the white of her hair and faintly bluish white of face and hands all is black. For an eye having no need of light to see. All this in the present as had she the misfortune to be still of this world.
>
> (Beckett 2010: 451)

She hears the howls of laughter of the dead who are damned but in spite of this still treasures her memories. All the while she is firmly in the present experiencing things like her breathing and her old hands. When she finally decides to let go of life and compares it to licking one's lips after the last morsel of food at a meal, she finally knows happiness:

> Decision no sooner reached or rather long after than what is the wrong word? For the last time at last for to end yet again what the wrong word? Than [sic] revoked. No but slowly dispelled a little very little like the last wisps of day when the curtain closes. Of itself by slow millimetres or drawn by a phantom hand. Farewell to farewell. Then in that perfect dark foreknell darling sound pip for end begun. First last moment. Grant only enough remain to devour all. Moment by glutton moment. Sky earth the whole kit and boodle. Not another crumb of carrion left. Lick chops and basta. No. One last. Grace to breathe that void. Know happiness.
> (Beckett 2010: 470)

Of this passage, Badiou writes 'the instant of happiness is reached in the very brief, laborious time of the visitation of the void' (Badiou 2008b: 284). Moreover, writes Badiou, in it we see 'in art the passage from the misfortune of life and of the visible to the happiness of a veridical incitement of the void' (Badiou 2008b: 284). Finally, it beautifully ties together many of the earlier discussed themes: 'It requires the immeasurable power of the encounter; it requires the wager of a nomination; it requires the combinations of wandering and fixity, of the imperative and the tale' (Badiou 2008b: 284).

These themes are rendered even more powerful in *Ill Seen Ill Said* because of the style of Beckett's modernist prose. Arguably, the full power of her encounter with the void is only available through prose that mirrors the coincidence of opposites of a being that is both fixed (her body lies 'on' a bed) and wandering (her mind travels 'on' in the void). The syntactical centre and precise point of grammatical control over this encounter is located in the preposition 'on' used by Beckett as a repeated sentence. This simple one-word prepositional-sentence also captures well the combination of 'the tale' of the old woman and 'the imperative' of the story. Each can be metaphysically condensed and stylistically rendered into this one-word sentence: 'On'.

Beckett takes the encounter to the heights of modernist literature. Moreover, characters like Beckett's old woman and scenes in darkness from the void rendered through innovative (and difficult) prose are not uncommon in his fiction and drama. Nevertheless, as a depiction of a dose of despair as the condition of real happiness, there is perhaps not a better source text in Beckett's oeuvre. Badiou hits on the reason for this by pointing out that the entire beginning *Ill Seen Ill Said* pivots around the word 'unhappiness', 'whereas the end trends towards the word "happiness"' (Badiou 2008b: 283). What happens between the journey from 'unhappiness' to 'happiness'

> is that if, at the start, we set out in the reign of visibility and the rigidity of seeing in the nocturnal grey (in limbo between life and death), at the end a sort of light void readies in the second nocturne.
>
> (Badiou 2008b: 283)

Overall, Beckett's writing is connected to antiphilosophers such as Pascal and Kierkegaard for Badiou because of its focus on the despair of human existence. However, regarding Beckett's approach to humanity, Badiou finds in it a 'functional reduction of humanity' wherein it is 'treated as something that is oriented towards essence, or Idea', that is to say, metaphysics (Badiou 2008b: 254). According to Badiou, Beckett develops this metaphysics by exploring, among other things, 'the processes by which the subject might hope to identify itself', the possibilities of naming 'what happens or arrives *insofar as* it arrives', and the '*existence of the Two*, or the virtuality of the Other' (Badiou 2008b: 254). The latter issue is important as a site of possibility for going beyond *solipsism*, that is, a position in metaphysics that the individual self is the whole of reality. In turn, this opens up the possibility of loving someone other than one's own self.

Finally, for Badiou, in

> the numericity of love (as one, two, infinity) is the place of what Beckett, quite rightly, called happiness. Happiness also singularizes the amorous procedure, there is only happiness in love; it is the reward specific to this type of truth. There is pleasure in art, joy in science and enthusiasm in politics, but in love there is happiness.
>
> (Badiou 2008b: 282)

In specific, the numericity of love, and thus, happiness, in Beckett is as follows:

> In love, there is first the One of solipsism, which consists in the confrontation or the body-to-body of the cogito and black-grey of being in the infinite repetition (*ressassement*) of speech. Then there is the Two, which occurs in the event of the encounter and in the incalculable poem of its naming. And last, there is the Infinite of the sensible which the Two traverses and develops, and in which it little

> by little deciphers a truth of the Two itself. This numericity—one, two, infinity—is specific to the amorous procedure.
>
> (Badiou 2008b: 281–82)

If Badiou's thoughts here on the numericity of love in Beckett are directed towards *Ill Seen Ill Said*, the happiness found by the old woman might also be described as love. The One of her solipsism consists of her lying on her bed infinitely (i.e. 'On' and 'On') caught in the repetition of her thoughts. Then, there is the Two which occurs in the event of her encounter with the void and the 'incalculable' poem of its naming: a naming captured beautifully in the lines, 'Decision no sooner reached or rather long after than what is the wrong word? For the last time at last for to end yet again what the wrong word?' These lines depict her efforts at nomination, one that moves from 'what *is* the wrong word' (my emphasis) to the copula-less syntactic formation, 'what the wrong word'. Her metaphysical struggle here moves towards the Infinite when the 'is' of being, the copula, is removed from the syntactic structure of her nomination process, and she finally begins to decipher a truth of the Two itself, namely, knowledge of happiness (Know happiness). In sum, Badiou finds that the form and style of Beckett's literary art perfectly exemplifies the antiphilosophical idea that 'a certain dose of despair is the condition of real happiness' (Badiou 2019: 72)—a condition that is also subject to the numericity of love.

Happiness and affect

Badiou argues that happiness is integral to philosophy. Moreover, he claims that the life of the philosopher is the *happiest* life. But this was not a position that he has held throughout his long and illustrious philosophical career. Rather, it is a position he first defended in a book on happiness that he published a couple of years before he turned 80. Prior to this, Badiou held that philosophy will:

1. Envisage love solely according to the truth that hatches on the Two of sexuation, and on the Two of *tout court. But without* the tension of pleasure-displeasure kept in play by the love-object.
2. Envisage politics as truth of the infinite of collective situations, as a treatment in truth of this infinite, *but without* the enthusiasm or sublimity of these situations themselves.
3. Envisage mathematics as a truth of multiple-being in and through the letter, as a power of literalisation, *but without* the intellectual beatitude of the resolved problem.

4 And last envisage the poem as a truth of sensible presence lodged in rhythm and image *but without* the corporeal capitation of rhythm and image (Badiou 2008c: 44; my emphasis).

The emphasised words 'but without' signify the detachment of philosophy from any affect or set of affects. Philosophy here deals with truth, not the *affects* of truth. Whereas the general meaning of 'affect' is a sensation or a feeling, for Badiou it means something more than this. It is also 'an effect of subjective experimental reasoning in a particular genre', which is 'a highly rigorous and restricted conception of affect' (Bartlett and Clemens 2019: 11).

Nevertheless, while philosophy had no affect for the greater part of Badiou's career (which we saw earlier in his comments on Mallarme's Constellation), it takes on a very specific affect much later in his career. To provide philosophy with an affect, Badiou finds it

> necessary to introduce here a sharp distinction between 'happiness' and 'satisfaction'. I am satisfied when I see that my individual interests are in conformity with what the world has to offer. Satisfaction is thereby determined by the laws of the world and by the harmony between these laws and myself. Ultimately, I am satisfied when I can be assured that I am well integrated with the world.
> (Badiou 2019: 87–88)

Thus, for Badiou, satisfaction is associable with Freud's death drive and 'is in reality a form of subjective death, because the individual, reduced to its conformity with the world as it is, is incapable of becoming the generic subject that it is capable of being' (Badiou 2019: 88). In contradistinction to satisfaction, 'happiness is on the side of affirmation, of creation, of the new, and of genericity' (Badiou 2019: 88). Badiou rightly claims that he is '*inventing a new form of happiness* which is a victory over the dictatorship and the power of the death drive' (Badiou 2019: 88; my emphasis). This new form of happiness disassociates it with the other 'happiness', the one that is the object of Freudian, Lacanian, *and* Žižekian critique, and associated with satisfaction in consumer culture. In short, 'satisfaction' is the 'happiness' that is guaranteed and comes without risk; whereas 'happiness'—or what Badiou calls 'real happiness' to distinguish it from the happiness of fantasy—is not guaranteed and comes with risk.

As such, this new form of happiness that Badiou invents has an incredible power over the world—*the power to change the world.* It does this through its metaphysical, not its social potential:

> Happiness is not the possibility of the satisfaction of everyone. Happiness is not the abstract idea of a good society in which everyone is satisfied. Happiness is the subjectivity of a difficult task: coping with the consequences of an event and discovering, beneath the dull and dreary existence of our world, the luminous possibilities offered by the affirmative real, of which the law of this world was the hidden negation. Happiness is enjoying the powerful and creative existence of something that, from the world's point of view, was impossible.
>
> (Badiou 2019: 89)

Badiou caps this passage off with two lines that are both 'truly encouraging' and extremely powerful for the practice of philosophy: 'How to change the world? The response is truly encouraging: by being happy' (Badiou 2019: 89). But make no mistake: the conditions of this type of new happiness are rigorous and demanding though not impossible.

In Abderrahmane Sissako's film, *Waiting for Happiness* (*Heremakono: En attendant le bonheur*, 2002), the luminous possibilities for real happiness are beautifully depicted in the relationship between Khatra (Khatra Ould Abdel Kader), a young orphan boy of about nine years of age, and the elderly Maata (Maata Ould Mohamed Abeid). Maata, an electrician who has adopted Khatra, mentors the boy in his trade. Together they bring electrical power and light to customers in the Mauritanian port city of Nouadhibou. But in addition to dialogue on why a particular light bulb setup that they have installed does not work, they also talk a lot about death. Prompted by Khatra, who asks the elderly man frequently the same question, 'Maata, are you afraid of death?' Maata regularly replies that he is not. The communication of technical (electricity) and philosophical (death) knowledge between the elderly man and the young boy establishes the importance of good communication: it is literally and figuratively a matter of life and death. Maata is insistent that the boy learns the lessons he needs to impart to him so that when he dies, the boy can carry on with his life; Khatra is equally insistent that the elderly man share his wisdom on death. The biopolitics at the heart of their exchanges is beautifully understated to the point where one feels that they are exchanging nothing less than eternal truths on life and death.

The philosophical affect in these scenes is remarkable and reminiscent of Badiou's new form of happiness that he says is a victory over the power of the death drive. This affect is most evident after the passing of Maata. In a touch of biopolitical magical realism, the light bulb that did not work all of sudden does after Maata dies. Then, there is also the light bulb that washes to shore and the one held by the dying Maata—both emphasising literally and figuratively the consequences of successful communication: a deeper knowledge of light *and* darkness. This deeper knowledge is that even with a good bulb and sufficient power, sometimes the bulb does not produce light—an insight that alludes to the greater metaphysical mysteries of both life and death. The scenes of Khatra after the death of Maata reveal the boy to have learned the difference between satisfaction and real happiness described by Badiou: not only does he cope with the consequences of the death of Maata, he appears to have discovered 'luminious possibilities'—heavily symbolised by Sissako's light bulbs—'beneath the dull dreary existence of our world'. The effect of happiness is established in Khatra's enjoyment of 'the powerful and creative existence of something that, from the world's point of view, was impossible': the illumination of light bulbs without electricity.

Moreover, in the hands of Sissako, film is less a narrative form than a *poetic* one. 'For me', says Sissako agreeing to the poetic quality of this film,

> poetry is a better way to communicate with the other, to say things that are important, that are important politically because when we live in a country, and on a continent where making a film is a very rare and difficult act because the means are not so readily available, we can only be but political. But political in the sense of building a better world, but not only for oneself but for everyone.
> (Scarlet 2007: n.p.)

As such, we might then take the liberty of drawing on Badiou one last time by regarding *Waiting for Happiness* as poetic *political* philosophy, that is, 'as a truth of sensible presence lodged in rhythm and image'. In short, by reading into the film Badiou's distinction between satisfaction and real happiness, the luminous possibilities of *Waiting for Happiness* appear as nothing less than the possibilities of real happiness.

Badiou's real happiness is not a product that can bought and sold in the free market as the happiness industry would have us believe. Rather, it comes from a recognition of the kind of 'satisfaction' that comes from living in harmony with the laws of the world versus the real 'happiness' that he calls 'the *jouissance* of the impossible' (Badiou 2019: 85). For him, it is a *jouissance* that stems from 'acts, creations, organizations and thoughts which accept the new and radical possibility of that whose impossibility was a law of the world' (Badiou 2019: 85).

Real happiness also involves being faithful to becoming the subject of change—it is a *fidelity* that comes with all real happiness.

In our own time, a philosophy that locates happiness in *changing* the world as opposed to finding one's place in it is truly revolutionary. It allows us to locate both happiness *and* philosophy in encounters ranging from scientific knowledge to mass protests. Writes Badiou,

> All philosophy—even and above all when it is supported by complex scientific knowledges, innovative works of art, revolutionary politics, intense loves—is a metaphysics of happiness, or it's not worth an hour of our trouble. For why impose on thought and life the formidable tests of demonstration, the general logic of thinking, the intelligence of formalisms, the attentive reading of recent poems, the risky engagement in mass rallies, love without guarantee, if it is not because this is necessary for true life finally to exist—that which Rimbaud said is absent, and of which we maintain, we philosophers who repudiate all forms of skepticism, cynicism, relativism and the shallow irony of the non-dupes, that true life can never be totally absent?
>
> (Badiou 2019: 36)

What also should be apparent from Badiou's thoughts on real happiness is that the practice of real philosophy is itself life affirming. Moreover, the practice of Badiou's form of philosophy whose affects are real happiness is not limited to formalising arguments or climbing truth trees. Rather, acts such as attentively reading literature and engaging in rallies always hold the potential of real happiness if approached philosophically. This position is very different from that of Barthes where reading literature can result in *jouissance* but can only change our individual lives, not the world.

It is telling that Badiou reminds us that Spinoza had an even 'stronger' word for happiness: *beatitudo*. Why? Because now that he has brought the concept of happiness into his philosophical system, he strives to endow it with a power on the level it held in Spinoza's system. But, as with Pascal where Badiou adopts his wager without God, so too with Spinoza: it is *beatitudo* without God. This is a huge shift as Spinoza's *beatitudo* is predicated (through proof) upon the existence of God. Moreover, it is alternately translated as 'happiness', 'salvation', and 'blessedness'.

This is important to recall because Badiou reminds us that for Spinoza, 'Happiness is not the reward of virtue, but virtue itself' (Badiou 2019: 35). Badiou glosses this famous line from Spinoza's *Ethics*, which first appeared in 1677, the year of his death, as saying 'Happiness is the affect of the True, which could not have existed were it not for mathematics, and could not have been concentrated in an intuition if it had not first been demonstrated' (Badiou 2019: 35–36).[1] But these lines have very different connotations when 'salvation' and 'blessedness' are substituted for 'happiness'.

If we look at another translation of this line from Spinoza's *Ethics* within the context of the lines that follow it, we see how 'happiness' renders different connotations than 'blessedness':

> Proposition 42
>
> Blessedness is not the reward of virtue, but virtue itself. We do not enjoy blessedness because we keep our lusts in check. On the contrary, it is because we enjoy blessedness that we are able to keep our lusts in check.
>
> Proof
>
> Blessedness consists in love towards God (Pr. 36,V and Sch.), a love that arises from the third kind of knowledge (Cor.Pr.32,V), and so this love (Prs.59 and 3,III) must be related to the mind in so far as the mind is active; and there it is virtue itself (Def.8,IV). That is the first point. Again, the more the mind enjoys this divine love or blessedness, the more it understands (Pr.32,V); that is (Cor. Pr.3,V), the more power it has over the emotions and (Pr.38,V) the less subject it is to emotions that are bad. So the mind's enjoyment of this divine love or blessedness gives it the power to check lusts. And since human power to keep lusts in check consists solely in the intellect, nobody enjoys blessedness because he has kept his emotions in check. On the contrary, the power to keep lusts in check arises from blessedness itself.
>
> (Spinoza 1982: 225)

Spinoza saw the emotions as something that could be studied in the same way that we study geometry or physics. Hence, his *Ethics* utilises a geometric method of demonstration and proof employing a variety of definitions, explications, axioms, propositions, proofs, corollaries, scholia. Above we see a proposition followed by part of its 'proof' in which are nested references to previously established propositions ('Pr'.), scholia ('Sch'.), and corollaries ('Cor'.). By the time you reach Proposition 42, you are looking at the last proposition of the final part (V) of Spinoza's *Ethics*. *Beatitudo* is only possible *because* of the existence of God, or, as the proof above states, it 'consists in love towards God'. And God's existence was proven way back in the first part of the *Ethics*. In short, without the existence of God, there is no *beatitudo* for Spinoza; likewise, without *philosophy*, there is no 'real' happiness for Badiou.

Beatitudo, for Spinoza, is linked with freeing ourselves from the bondage of our passive emotions, and the attainment of knowledge of our place in the universe. This knowledge shows us why things happen in the ways they do happen and cannot be otherwise. For Spinoza, this brings us both happiness and salvation. Most people are servants to passion and emotion because they lack knowledge. However, for Spinoza, virtue is *power*. It is our capacity to act from understanding and is something that implies a certain level of knowledge. The final part of the Spinoza's *Ethics* shows us how through virtue we can free ourselves from the bondage of passion. Happiness requires that we understand the nature of particular emotions so that we may free ourselves from their bondage.

For Spinoza, self-understanding requires that we understand that we are a particular mode within God (or Nature, which as one substance, makes God and Nature co-extensive). Thus, knowledge of oneself is also knowledge of God. But as love is an *affect* that involves knowledge, to know is to love God. Thus, the more we come to know through self-knowledge, the more we come to both know and love God. Moreover, for Spinoza, 'the highest good', or, the *summum bonum* (a Latin phrase Spinoza uses which was introduced by Cicero) is this love of God. It is also that which, as stated in Proposition 42 above, brings us happiness (or 'blessedness').

While these comments on happiness in Spinoza just scratch the surface of his great metaphysical system, they are enough to establish a link between Badiou's notion of affect, happiness, and philosophy, and the work of this so-called God-intoxicated philosopher. Again, the road to happiness in Badiou's philosophy borrows heavily from theological philosophy to produce a new form of revolutionary, albeit secular, happiness. To say then as Žižek does that happiness is a category of 'mere being' for Badiou, one which is also 'confused, indeterminate, inconsistent', no longer holds. Perhaps too it never held because it was only fairly recently that Badiou worked out his metaphysics of happiness: a metaphysics with the power to change the world.

Conclusion

Badiou's happiness calls for us to never settle for the place we have been assigned in the world. Rather, it encourages a restlessness and risk that strive to change the world and our place in it. By distinguishing 'satisfaction' from 'happiness' he further distances his own position on happiness from both the philosophical tradition dating back to the Greeks and Romans *and* the happiness that is the subject of critique of the psychoanalytic tradition. Real happiness is adventurous and spontaneous, whereas its other, the happiness of fantasy (or what he calls 'satisfaction'), is one that is guaranteed through the products and processes of the happiness industry.

Moreover, by making real happiness the province of philosophy and its affects, Badiou is withdrawing happiness from the everyday dialectic between satisfaction and dissatisfaction. To be satisfied or not *is not* a question of happiness. Rather, the question of happiness lies in the questions and relations of the true life—one that embraces possibilities and abhors impossibility. Still, Badiou is not saying that we can always change the world. Happiness is as prone to catastrophe as satisfaction. The catastrophes regarding happiness though are of different orders: 'some result from tiredness and surrender', says Badiou, 'whereas others are from disloyalty or betrayal' (Badiou n.d.). 'In my philosophy', he continues, 'evil is the fact of being subjectively responsible for a catastrophe of happiness' (Badiou n.d.). For Badiou, the experience of catastrophes of happiness, which he also calls 'disasters', is as terrible as the experience of happiness is intense. He also says that conservatives like these catastrophes of happiness because they provide the 'main argument for *settling* for satisfaction' (Badiou n.d.; my emphasis).

Aside from the literary sources of Badiou's notion of happiness in writers ranging from Mallarmé to Beckett, and the philosophical ones in the antiphilosophies of thinkers such as Pascal and Kierkegaard, there is an elaborate meta-mathematical metaphysics that underlies his theory of happiness. It is no less complex and well-structured than Spinoza's elaborate geometrical proofs for the existence of God which make possible *beatitude*. Badiou's metaphysical system is founded upon specific developments in mathematics, namely, the paradoxes of Set Theory (as established by Gottlob Frege and Bertrand Russell) and their axiomatic resolution (as established by Ernest Zermelo and Abraham Fraenkel, John von Neumann, and Kurt Gödel). These are both beautiful and unlikely sources, a fact illustrated most directly in Russell's *The Conquest of Happiness* (1930), which explores the causes of happiness and unhappiness with no indirect or direct reference to his own set theory. Badiou's philosophical genius lies in his ability not only to produce a revolutionary theory of happiness but also to establish it as an extension (or corollary, if you will) of his own metaphysics. Something that not even the great analytic philosopher was able to achieve. A theory of happiness that advocates the pursuit of philosophy as the true life of the revolutionary is a welcome reprieve from a world that is everywhere turning its back on philosophy, happiness, and truth.

But the value of Badiou's contributions to a theory of happiness goes beyond just reestablishing the significance of philosophy and happiness in the world today. They also arguably provide literature with a much more exalted significance than the happiness industry, the psychoanalytic critique of happiness, and aesthetic hedonism. As you will recall, the happiness industry and positive psychology are not interested in knowledge and truth, particularly when they cut into the profits of airport book sales and TED talks by its authors. Its associated literature is essentially a marketing and promotional arm of the corporate publishing industry, wherein the importance of literature is primarily based on its sales figures. The tragic view of happiness *is* interested in knowledge and truth *but* uses this as a basis to reject happiness. The work of these proponents of the tragic view of happiness can be linked to the downfall of global capital by progressive theorists. Its associated literature exalts the virtues of knowledge and truth in the name of desire, and though cherished by readers who are comfortable with rejecting a life of happiness, is relatively limited in its sales potential and antithetical to the ends of corporate publishing. Aesthetic hedonism offers an alternative to both the approach of the happiness industry and the tragic view by redirecting questions of the pursuit—and non-pursuit—of happiness towards the dual arts of textuality and living. Its associated literature is broad and wide, and only limited by the possibilities of the *plaisir* and *jouissance* of textuality. Barthes's hedonism incorporates into its theoretical purview a pluralistic range of literature that includes the combined literature of the happiness industry and the tragic view of literature.

While each of these three distinct paths to understanding the status of literature with regard to happiness have their merits, each pales when compared to the exalted role of literature in Badiou's theory of happiness. Whereas the happiness industry affords literature with the power to make people happy, and the tragic view of happiness shows how literature can reveal to us the truth of our desire, and aesthetic hedonism offers literature a role in the moral life, none of these paths has the revolutionary power to change the world *and* afford opportunities for *real* happiness and a *true* life. The importance of literature in Badiou is seen not just in the way the modernist writings of Mallarmé and Beckett serve as metaphysical resources for his philosophical vision of happiness, but rather the way the work of literature can and does function metaphysically as foundational and fundamental thinking. Moreover, to see these ideas carried out in the poetry of an African film should only further encourage examination of the role of literature and the other arts with respect to progressive visions of happiness in texts from all over the world. What links Beckett's old woman and Sissako's young man is the achievement of happiness through metaphysical, not financial, wealth. Philosophical affect with regard to happiness as presented by Badiou has the power to cross economic, cultural, and social divides. Perhaps this is ultimately its *real* revolutionary power.

If the politics of happiness in the eighteenth century brought literature and philosophy closer together in collaboration of the pursuit of happiness, then the economics of happiness in the twenty-first century has pushed apart literature and theory over the knowledge and truth claims of happiness. In the work of Badiou, however, there is the promise of philosophy and literature collaborating in the pursuit of not *mere* happiness, but *real* happiness.

While it may be premature to say that 'happiness is *again* a new idea' in Badiou, there are reasons to believe this, particularly *after* its industrialisation and dismissal have dominated twentieth-century thought. *Brave New World* integrated current theory to posit a dystopic future for society with regard to happiness. Maybe instead of regarding this novel a century later as predicting fairly accurately the contemporary world, we should regard the theories of Ford, Freud, and Wells that dominated it as incapable of providing *real* happiness and *true* life in the future—and look to new theories such Badiou's as a template for reassessing the future of happiness and its potential to change the standing of literature and save the world from catastrophe.

Note

1 Bartlett and Clemens change the Curley translation of Spinoza (1996: 180) from 'blessedness' to 'happiness', 'to keep it in line with Badiou's terminology and remarks' (Badiou 2019: 35fn1).

Bibliography

Alain (1989), *Alain on Happiness*, trans. Robert D. and Jane E. Cottrell, Evanston, IL: Northwestern University Press.

Aristotle (1941), *Nicomachean Ethics*, in *The Basic Works of Aristotle*, ed. Richard McKeon, trans. W. D. Ross, New York: Random House, pp. 935–1126.

Augustine, Saint (1961), *Confessions*, trans. R. S. Pine-Coffin, New York: Penguin.

Badiou, Alain (1990), 'Saisissement, dessaisie, fidélité', *Les Temps modernes* 531.33: 14–22.

Badiou, Alain [1989] (2008b), 'The Writing of the Generic', in *Conditions* [1992], trans. Steven Corcoran, London: Continuum, pp. 251–284.

Badiou, Alain [1992] (2008c), 'The Philosophical Recourse of the Poem', in *Conditions* [1992], pp. 35–48.

Badiou, Alain [1990] (2012), 'Commitment, Detachment, Fidelity', in *The Adventure of French Philosophy*, ed. and trans. Bruno Bosteels, London: Verso, pp. 27–38.

Badiou, Alain [2015] (2019), *Happiness*, trans. A. J. Bartlett and Justin Clemens, London: Bloomsbury.

Badiou, Alain [n.d.], 'Interview with Nicholas Truong', trans. David Broder, http://www.versobooks.com/blogs/2192-badiou-s-happiness-lesson.

Barthes, Roland (1970), *S/Z*, Paris: Seuil.

Barthes, Roland [1973] (1975), *The Pleasure of the Text*, trans. Richard Howard, New York: Hill and Wang.

Barthes, Roland [1971] (1976), *Sade/Fourier/Loyola*, trans. Richard Miller, New York: Hill and Wang.

Barthes, Roland [1975] (1977), *Roland Barthes by Roland Barthes*, trans. Richard Howard, New York: Hill and Wang.

Barthes, Roland [1942] (1982), 'On Gide and His Journal', *A Barthes Reader*, ed. Susan Sontag, trans. Richard Howard, New York: Hill and Wang, pp. 3–17.

Barthes, Roland [1987] (2010), *Incidents*, trans. Teresa Fagen, London: Seagull.

Barthes, Roland [2015] (2018), *Album*, trans. Jody Gladding, ed. Éric Marty, New York: Columbia University Press.

Bartlett, Adam John and Justin Clemens (2019), 'Translators' Foreword', in Alain Badiou, *Happiness*, pp. 1–32.
Beckett, Samuel [1981] (2010), '*Ill Seen Ill Said*', in *The Selected Works of Samuel Beckett*, volume four, ed. Paul Auster, New York: Grove, pp. 451–470.
Beiser, Frederick C. (2014), *After Hegel*, Princeton, NJ: Princeton University Press.
Bentham, Jeremy (1839), *Principles of Judicial Procedure*, in *The Works of Jeremy Bentham*, part VII, Edinburgh: William Tait.
Bentham, Jeremy (1843), 'Pannomial Fragments', in *The Works of Jeremy Bentham*, volume III, Edinburgh: William Tait, pp. 211–232.
Bentham, Jeremy [1780] (1879), *An Introduction to the Principles of Morals and Legislation*, Oxford: Clarendon Press.
Bentham, Jeremy (2011), *Selected Writings*, ed. Stephen G. Engelmann, New Haven, CT: Yale University Press.
Black Mirror (2017), 'Arkangel', season 4, episode 2, dir. Jodie Foster, Netflix, December 29.
Bowie, David (1974a), *1984*, US Single, RCA (JH-10026) Mono.
Bowie, David (1974b), *Diamond Dogs*, US LP, RCA (APL1–0576).
Bradshaw, David (1994), 'Introduction', in *The Hidden Huxley*, ed. David Bradshaw, London: Faber and Faber, pp. vii–xxvi.
Bruckner, Pascal (2006), 'Happiness', in *The Columbia History of Twentieth-Century French Thought*, ed. Lawrence Kritzman, New York: Columbia University Press, pp. 242–245.
Catmantoo (2014), 'Happy Dogs & Cat in Australia', YouTube, 2:58, May 1, https://www.youtube.com/watch?time_continue=19&v=DePFiF-nNoE&-feature=emb_logo.
Chiesa, Lorenzo (2006), 'Lacan with Artaud', in *Lacan*, ed. Slavoj Žižek, London: Verso, pp. 336–364.
Culler, Jonanthan [1983] (2002), *Barthes*, Oxford: Oxford University Press.
'Cyrenaics' (1910), *Encyclopedia Britannica, Eleventh Edition*, volume VII, New York: Encyclopedia Britannica Company, pp. 703–704.
Davies, William (2015), *The Happiness Industry*, London: Verso.
Déclaration des droits de l'homme et du citoyen (1789), 26 August, http://www.refworld.org/docid/3ae6b4ec28.html.
Declaration of the Right of Man and the Citizen (1789), 26 August, https://www.refworld.org/docid/3ae6b52410.html.
Dehghan, Saeed (2014), 'Iranian Pharrell Williams Fans Behind Happy Video Sentenced', *The Guardian*, September 19, https://www.theguardian.com/world/2014/sep/19/iranian-pharrell-williams-fans-happy-video-sentenced.
Descartes, René [1641] (1967), 'Meditations on the First Philosophy', in *The Philosophical Works of Descartes*, two vols., trans. Elizabeth Haldane and G. R. T. Ross, Cambridge: Cambridge University Press, vol. 1, pp. 132–199.
Despicable Me 2 (2013), dir. Pierre Coffin and Chris Renaud, Universal Pictures, film.
Eurythmics (1984), *1984 (For the Love of Big Brother)*, US LP, RCA (ABL1–5349).

Foucault, Michel (2010), *The Government of the Self and Others: Lectures at the Collège de France, 1982–1983*, trans. Graham Burchell, New York: Palgrave Macmillan.

Frenz, Horst (ed.) (1969), "André Gide, Literature 1947," in *Nobel Lectures, Literature 1901–1967*, Amsterdam: Elsevier, pp. 421–429.

Freud, Sigmund [1940] (1949), *An Outline of Psychoanalysis*, trans. James Strachey, New York: W. W. Norton.

Freud, Sigmund [1920] (1950), *Beyond the Pleasure Principle*, trans. James Strachey, New York: Liveright.

Freud, Sigmund [1929] (1955), *Civilization and Its Discontents*, trans. Joan Riviere, London: Hogarth Press.

Freud, Sigmund [1933] (1965), 'Femininity', *New Introductory Lectures on Psychoanalysis*, trans. James Strachey, New York: W. W. Norton, pp. 112–135.

Freud, Sigmund [1895] (1966), 'Psychotherapy of Hysteria', in Sigmund Freud and Joseph Breuer, *Studies on Hysteria* [1895], ed. and trans. James Strachey, New York: Avon Books, pp. 299–352.

Gantt, Edwin (2000), 'Cognitive Psychology, Rationality, and the Assumption of Hedonism', *The General Psychologist* 35.3: 82–86.

Gide, André (1947–1951), *The Journals of André Gide: 1889–1949*, four vols., trans. Justin O'Brien, New York: Knopf.

Gide, André (1932), "Pages de journal," *La Nouvelle Revue Française* 225.1 (June): 985–1004.

Haybron, Daniel M. (2013), *Happiness*, Oxford: Oxford University Press.

Hazard, Paul [1946] (1963), *European Thought in the Eighteenth Century*, Cleveland: Meridian.

Hellman, John (1982), *Simone Weil*, Eugene, OR: Wipf and Stock.

Herodotus (1972), *The Histories*, trans. Aubrey de Sélincourt, New York: Penguin.

Horkheimer, Max, and Theodor W. Adorno [1944] (1972), *Dialectic of Enlightenment*, trans. John Cumming, New York: Seabury.

Horowitz, Daniel (2018), *Happier? The History of a Cultural Movement that Aspired to Transform America*, New York: Oxford University Press.

Howard, Richard (1975), 'A Note on the Text', in Roland Barthes, *The Pleasure of the Text*, pp. v–viii.

Hudson, Deal W. (1996), *Happiness and the Limits of Satisfaction*, Lanham, MD: Rowman & Littlefield.

Husserl, Edmund (1960), *Cartesian Meditations*, trans. Dorion Cairns, Boston: Martinus Nijhoff.

Huxley, Aldous [1932] (1956), *Brave New World*, CBS Radio Workshop, two episodes, 30 min. per episode, released January 27 and February 6.

Huxley, Aldous [1958] (1965), *Brave New World Revisited*, New York: Harper & Row.

Huxley, Aldous (1969), *Letters of Aldous Huxley*, ed. Grover Smith, New York: Harper & Row.

Huxley, Aldous [1932] (1980), *Brave New World*, dir. Burt Brinckerhoff, Universal Television, released March 7, 87 min., television film.

Huxley, Aldous [1934] (1994), 'What is Happening to our Population?', in *The Hidden Huxley*, ed. David Bradshaw, pp. 147–158.

Huxley, Aldous [1932] (1998), *Brave New World*, Universal Television, released April 19, 1h 27min., television film.

Huxley, Aldous [1932] (2001a), 'Are We Growing Stupider', in *Complete Essays: Volume 3*, eds. Robert Baker and James Sexton, Chicago, IL: Ivan R. Dee, pp. 323–324.

Huxley, Aldous [1927] (2001b), 'The Outlook for American Culture', *Complete Essays: Volume 3*, pp. 185–194.

Huxley, Aldous [1932] (2006), *Brave New World*, London: Harper.

Huxley, Aldous [1932] (2008), *Brave New World*, ten episodes, radio reading, BBC, first broadcast, https://www.bbc.co.uk/programmes/b00dpygl/episodes/guide.

Huxley, Aldous [1932] (2015), *Brave New World*, dir. James Dacre, Royal & Derngate Theatres (Northampton), premiered 4 September.

Huxley, Aldous [1932] (2016), *Brave New World*, two episodes, dir. David Hunter, BBC, released 28 May and 4 June, 58 min. each, television adaptation. https://www.bbc.co.uk/programmes/p03t5j58/p03t5d4q.

Huxley, Aldous [1932] (2020), *Brave New World*, season 1 (9 episodes), developed by David Wiener, Amblin Entertainment, premier episode 15 July 15 (Peacock).

iamOTHER (2013), 'Pharrell Williams–Happy', YouTube, 4:05, November 21, https://www.youtube.com/watch?time_continue=20&v=y6Sxv-sUYtM&-feature=emb_title. –

Ionescu, Ghita (1984), *Politics and the Pursuit of Happiness*, London: Longman.

Johnson, Samuel [1756] (1889), *Rasselas*, ed. Henry Morley, London: Cassell.

Kant, Immanuel [1785] (1949a), 'Foundations of the Metaphysics of Morals', in *Critique of Practical Reason and Other Writings,* ed. and trans. Lewis White Beck, Chicago, IL: University of Chicago Press, pp. 50–117.

Kant, Immanuel [1788] (1949b), *Critique of Practical Reason*, in *Critique of Practical Reason and Other Writings*, pp. 118–260.

Kogan, Vivian (2006), 'André Gide', in *The Columbia History of Twentieth-Century French Thought*, ed. Lawrence Kritzman, pp. 537–539.

Kolbert, Jack (1985), *The Worlds of André Maurois*, Selinsgrove, PA: Susquehanna University Press.

Kosoff, Maya [n.d.], 'Pharrell Made only $2,700 in Songwriter Royalties', *Business Insider*, https://www.businessinsider.com/pharrell-made-only-2700-in-songwriter-royalties-from-43-million-plays-of-happy-on-pandora-2014-12.

Lacan, Jacques [1958] (1977a), 'The Direction of the Treatment and the Principles of Its Power', in *Écrits*, trans. Alan Sheridan, New York: W. W. Norton, pp. 226–280.

Lacan, Jacques [1953] (1977b), 'Function and Field of Speech and Language', in *Écrits*, pp. 30–113.

Lacan, Jacques [1955] (1977c), 'The Freudian Thing', in *Écrits*, pp. 114–145.

Lacan, Jacques (1997), *The Seminar of Jacques Lacan, Book VII*, trans. Dennis Porter, London: W. W. Norton.

Laertius, Diogenes (1925), 'Life of Aristippus', in *The Lives and Opinions of Eminent Philosophers, Books 1–5*, trans. R. D. Hicks, Cambridge, MA: Harvard University Press.

Larkin, Pascal (1930), *Property in the Eighteenth Century*, Cork.

Lateef, Yusef (1965), *1984*, US LP. Impulse! (A-84) Mono.

Lee, Ashley (2017), 'Why Broadway's "1984" Audiences Are Fainting, Vomiting and Getting Arrested', *Hollywood Reporter*, June 24, https://www.hollywoodreporter.com/news/why-broadways-1984-audiences-are-fainting-vomiting-getting-arrested-1016534.

Locke, John [1690] (1975), *An Essay Concerning Human Understanding*, ed. Peter H. Nidditch, Oxford: Oxford University Press.

Maazel, Lorin (2005), *1984*, premier May 3, Royal Opera House, Covent Garden, opera.

Mackey, Robert (2014), 'Director of "Happy in Tehran" Video is Reportedly Freed', *The New York Times*, May 29, https://www.nytimes.com/2014/05/30/world/middleeast/director-of-happy-in-tehran-video-is-reportedly-freed.html.

Mallarmé, Stéphane [1897] (1994), *Un Coup de Dés*, in *Collected Poems*, trans. Henry Weinfield, Berkeley: University of California Press, pp. 119–145.

Marty, Éric (2018), 'A Throw of the Dice,' *Memento by Diptyque (Paris)*, September 17, http://www.diptyqueparis-memento.com/en/a-throw-of-the-dice/.

Maurois, André (1950), *Alain*, Paris: Editions Domat.

McHendry, George F. (2019), 'Arkangel: Postscript on Families of Control', in *Through the Black Mirror*, eds. Terence McSweeney and Stuart Joy, New York: Palgrave Macmillan, pp. 205–216.

McMahon, Darrin M. (2006), *Happiness*, New York: Atlantic Monthly Press.

Mill, John Stuart [1873] (1957), *Autobiography*, New York: Liberal Arts Press.

Mill, John Stuart [1867] (1976), *Utilitarianism*, in *Utilitarianism, On Liberty,* and *Considerations on Representative Government,* ed. H. B. Acton, London: J. M. Dent.

Moriarty, Michael (2020), *Pascal*, Oxford: Oxford University Press.

Morris, Nigel (2012), 'Keeping It All in the (Nuclear) Family', *Frames Cinema Journal*, November 21, http://framescinemajournal.com/article/keeping-it-all-in-the-nuclear-family-big-brother-auntie-bbc-uncle-sam-and-george-orwells-nineteen-eighty-four/.

Norton, Brian Michael (2008), 'After the Summum Bonum', *Theory and Practice in the Eighteenth Century*, eds. Alexander Dick and Christina Lupton, London: Pickering and Chatto, pp. 211–223.

Oingo Boingo (1983), *Wake Up (It's 1984)*, US Single, A&M Records (AM-2610).

Orwell, George [1949] (1953), *Nineteen Eighty-four*, season 6, episode 1, dir. Paul Nickell, CBS, September 21, television.

Orwell, George [1949] (1954), *Nineteen Eighty-four*, dir. Rudolph Cartier, BBC, television.

Orwell, George [1949] (1956), *Nineteen Eighty-four*, dir. Michael Anderson, Holiday Film Productions, film.

Orwell, George [1949] (1984), *Nineteen Eighty-four*, dir. Michael Radford, Virgin Films, film.

Orwell, George [1949] (2013), *Nineteen Eighty-four*, adapted by Robert Icke and Duncan Macmillan. London: Bloomsbury.

Pascal, Blaise (1932), *Pensées*, trans. William Trotter, London: J. M. Dent.

Peardon, Thomas P. (1952), 'Introduction', in John Locke, *The Second Treatise of Government [1690]*, Indianapolis: Bobbs-Merrill, pp. vii–xxii.

Plottel, Jeanine (2006), 'Alain (Émile Chartier)', in *The Columbia History of Twentieth-Century French Thought*, ed. Lawrence Kritzman, pp. 379–380.

Pollard, Patrick (1991), *Gide*, London: Yale University Press.

Rasmussen, Eric Dean (2004), 'An Interview with Slavoj Žižek', *Electronic Book Review*, July 1, https://electronicbookreview.com/essay/liberation-hurts-an-interview-with-slavoj-zizek/.

Rettig, James (2014), '*Despicable Me 2* Rejected Pharrell 9 Times', *Stereogum*, December 4, https://www.stereogum.com/1723112/despicable-me-2-rejected-pharrell-9-times-before-he-made-them-happy/news/.

Richards, Keith, and James Fox (2010), *Life*, New York: Little Brown.

Rolling Stones (1972a), *Exile on Main Street*, UK LP (2), Rolling Stones Records (COC-69100).

Rolling Stones (1972b), *Happy*, US Single, Rolling Stones Records (RS-19104).

Rouhani, Hassan (@HassanRouhani) (2014), '#Happiness is our people's right', Twitter, May 21, 8:02 a.m., https://twitter.com/HassanRouhani/status/469100985798111232.

Rule, James Bernard (1997), *Theory and Progress in Social Science*, Cambridge: Cambridge University Press.

Saint-Just, Louis Antoine de (1984), *Oeuvres Completes*, Paris: Gérard Lebovici.

Samoyault, Tiphaine [2015] (2017), *Barthes*, trans. Andrew Brown, Malden, MA: Polity.

Sawyer, Dana (2002), *Aldous Huxley*, New York: Crossroad Publishing Company.

Scarlet, Peter [2006] (2007), 'Interview with Abderrahmane Sissako', in *Waiting for Happiness*, New Yorker Video, DVD.

Schopenhauer, Arthur [1883] (1957), *The World as Will and Idea*, three vols., trans. R. B. Haldane and J. Kemp, London: Routledge & Kegan Paul.

Shaw, Tamsin (2018), 'The New Military-Industrial Complex of Big Data Psy-Ops', *The New York Review of Books*, March 21, https://www.nybooks.com/daily/2018/03/21/the-digital-military-industrial-complex/.

Smith, Adam [1790] (2006), *The Theory of Moral Sentiments*, Mineola, NY: Dover.

Soloski, Alexis (2020), '"Brave New World" Arrives in the Future It Predicted', *New York Times*, July 13. https://www.nytimes.com/2020/07/13/arts/television/brave-new-world-peacock.html.

Sophocles (1972), *Oedipus the King*, trans. Anthony Burgess, Minneapolis: University of Minnesota Press.

Spinoza, Baruch (1982), *The Ethics*, trans. Samuel Shirley, Indianapolis: Hackett.

Spinoza, Baruch (1996), *The Ethics*, trans. Edwin Curley, London: Penguin.

Spirit (1969), *1984*, US Single, Ode Records (ZS7–128).

Strachey, James (1966), 'Editor's Introduction', in Sigmund Freud and Joseph Breuer, *Studies on Hysteria* [1895], ed. and trans. James Strachey, New York: Avon, pp. ix–xxix.

Szalai, Georg (2014), 'Pharrell Williams' "Happy" Becomes U.K.'s Most Downloaded Track Ever', *Hollywood Reporter*, September 10, https://www.hollywoodreporter.com/news/pharrell-williams-happy-becomes-uks-731828.

Tatranec Tatranský (2014), 'Pharrell Williams–HAPPY', YouTube, 4:03, March 18, https://www.youtube.com/watch?time_continue=79&v=sGrHwBlf7M&feature=emb_title.

Thody, Philip (1977), *Roland Barthes*, London: Macmillan.

#Trailer (2013), 'HAPPY–Pharrell Williams', YouTube, 4:05, June 28, https://www.youtube.com/watch?time_continue=14&v=MOWDb2TBYDg&feature=emb_logo.

Van Halen (1984), *1984*, US LP. Warner Bros (47741).

Voltaire [1759] (1947), *Candide*, trans. John Butt, Harmondsworth: Penguin.

Waiting for Happiness [2002] (2007), directed and written by Abderrahmane Sissako, Duo Films/ARTE France, New Yorker Video, DVD.

Wakeman, Rick (1981), *1984*, UK LP, Charisma (CDS-4022).

Watson, John B. (1913), 'Psychology as the Behaviorist Views It', *Psychological Review* 20.2: 158–177.

Watson, John B. (1925), *Behaviorism*, New York: W. W. Norton.

Weinfield, Henry (1994), '*Un Coup de Dés*: Commentary', in Stéphane Mallarmé, *Collected Poems*, pp. 264–275.

Weintraub, Steve (2012), 'Ridley Scott Talks *Prometheus*', *Collider*, May 31, https://collider.com/ridley-scott-prometheus-2-sequel-interview/170207/#more-170207.

Wellek, René (1992), *A History of Modern Criticism, Volume 8*, London: Yale University Press.

Williams, Pharrell (2013), 'Happy', Back Lot Music/I Am Other/Columbia, 7 inch record, 12 inch record, CD, and digital download, released November 21.

Williams, Pharrell (2014), *Girl*, US LP, Columbia (88843-05727-1)/I Am Other (88843-05727-1), released March 3.

Woiak, Joanne (2007), 'Designing a Brave New World', *The Public Historian* 29.3: 105–129.

Zalloua, Zahi (2020), *Žižek on Race*, New York: Bloomsbury.

Žižek, Slavoj (2001), *On Belief*, London: Routledge.

Žižek, Slavoj (2002), *Welcome to the Desert of the Real*, London: Verso.

Žižek, Slavoj (2005), *Interrogating the Real*, eds. Rex Butler and Scott Stephens, London: Continuum.

Žižek, Slavoj [1991] (2008a), *For They Know Not What They Do*, London: Verso.
Žižek, Slavoj (2008b), *In Defense of Lost Causes*, London: Routledge.
Žižek, Slavoj (2008c), *Violence*, New York: Picador.
Žižek, Slavoj (2009), *First as Tragedy, Then as Farce*, London: Verso.
Žižek, Slavoj (2012), 'Why Be Happy When You Could Be Interesting?', YouTube, 2:01, June 25, https://www.youtube.com/watch?v=U88jj6PSD7w.
Žižek, Slavoj (2014), *Event*, London: Penguin.
Žižek, Slavoj (2020), *A Left that Dares to Speak Its Name*, Medford, MA: Polity.
Žižek, Slavoj, and Jordan Peterson (2019), 'Happiness: Capitalism vs. Marxism', YouTube, 2:37:47, April 20, https://www.youtube.com/watch?v=pT1vutd4Gnk.

Index

Note: Page numbers followed by "n" denote endnotes.